Power vs. Poverty

Following the Money to Reveal America's Mass Incarceration Scheme

Rivera L. Peoples

Power vs. Poverty: Following the Money to Reveal America's Mass Incarceration Scheme

Cover Design: Shatorria Harris

ISBN: 9708364636096

Published in Nashville, Tennessee, *by BN Publication LLC*

Printed in the USA

DEDICATION

Kam, I hope this is even more proof that we can do anything we put our mind to if we work hard enough, no matter what. My biggest motivation is to be the best person and father I can be for you, Skylar and Zay, no matter where I am. Every day, I wish we were in the same room so I can see for myself how amazing you are. Until we get those moments again, keep being amazing and keep chasing all your dreams. That's the only way all mine come true. Love you.

I remain the same,
Yours

Skylar, my beautiful, beautiful Little attitude. You already know how much your dad loves you, and I'm so glad I do not have to prove that to anyone. I miss you more than I miss my freedom, honestly, and my heart belongs to you. It's important to me that you know you can do anything in this world if you work hard enough, stay focused, and believe in yourself more than anything else. You're growing into an amazing young lady. When you look in the mirror behind that beautiful smile, I hope you see all the strength you need to conquer this world.

I remain the same,
Yours

Ke'Zavier, when I think of you, I think of all the things I wish I would have done right, and then I think about all the things I hope and pray that go right for you.

Recognize your own potential. Do not limit yourself to what other people think of you. Be your own man and enjoy your journey in this life. Always be willing and determined to chase your dreams. One day, they will be your reality. Love you.

I remain the same,
Yours

This book is also dedicated to our next generation. I think it's irresponsible for us to focus *solely* on raising our own children the right way and continue to neglect society's most vulnerable, especially if the next little child growing up in poverty can ruin everything, we instilled in our own children by making them guilty by association of a crime or, worst, becoming a victim to violence of survival. (In order for there to be a suspect to keep locking up, there must be a victim). This book is dedicated to break generational curses of mass incarceration, even if I do it from the inside. My ultimate goal is for this book to bring effective change to the world of mass incarceration by using my own unique set of circumstances, before my kids, your kids, or our kids' friends, have to suffer in it.

"100 years from now it's not going to matter what your bank account was, the sort of house you lived in, or the kind of car you drove. What will matter is the effect we leave on our children."
  - anonymous

TABLE OF CONTENTS

FOREWORD BY E. KNOX

"Of all our studies, history is best qualified to reward our research. And when you see that you've got problems, all you have to do is examine the historical methods used all over the world by others who have problems similar to yours. And once you see how they got theirs straight, then you know how can get yours straight" -Malcolm X

To be afforded an opportunity to pen this foreword for *Power v. Poverty* was an honor, first and foremost. Rivera and I initially met inside of these soul-killing walls. We have now taken it upon ourselves to use these dehumanizing conditions and flip it -- flip it into our think tanks, our HIDDEN UNIVERSITY. With this new twenty-first century American social justice movement starting to awaken and challenge the plutocracy of this criminal justice system monster called "mass incarceration," *Power v. Poverty* is a continued conversation/thesis provoked by Michelle Alexander's *"The New Jim Crow."* For too long, there has been no mass fight back against the multi-evil assault on poor and vulnerable people, despite the heroic work of intellectual freedom fighters including Marian Wright Edelman, Angela Davis, Loïc Wacquant, Glenn Loury, Marc Mauer, and others. Yet, the sleepwalking is slowly but surely coming to a close as more and more fellow citizens realize that the iron cage they inhabit—maybe even a golden cage for the affluent—is still a form of bondage[1].

Incarcerated freedom fighters (past and present) Mamia Abujamaz, Larry B. Hoover, George Jackson, Gerrinmo Pratt, Tookie Williams, Steven Biko, Nelson Mandela, and many others have flipped their walls into their universities. Rivera and I both came from poverty-stricken environments. We were *fighting to live* then and, while living inside of these soul-killing walls, we are still *fighting to live.* The citizens of America that are in poverty, they're also fighting to live. Poverty steamrolls violence, which, in turn, justifies the war on us, the war on poverty, and the bogus war on drugs. One must first question, how is it that we got here and continue to be stuck here? Why are we, the people of color, mostly forced to act on a bestial state? Although slavery and Jim Crow semi- slavery era ended years ago, their legacies live on in various forms of structural racism. Contrary to popular notion about the concept of race, it is more than biological groupings. Race is about *financial, political, and social currencies.* Knowing the origin and nature of the value of race in this country in essential to many regarding the analysis of black America's dilemma. *It is important that blacks know why the race problem refuses to die, and how it is used to keep them and those equally affected by structural at a non-completive and powerless group*[2].

Brother Claud Anderson simply states it in layman's terms- so it can be easily understood - "true racism" exists only when one group holds a disproportionate share of wealth and power over another group, then uses these resources to marginalize, exploit, exclude, and subordinate the weaker group. [3]

A major way those of us incarcerated and our families have been, and continue to be, exploited and marginalized is the money transfer service and their fees being forced upon our families. Here in Tennessee, like in most states, the department of corrections utilizes JPay. Jpay is a financial service firm started by Ryan Shapiro, who was recently charged in federal court for conspiracy to commit securities fraud. Jpay was acquired in April 2015 by prison communications giant Securus Technologies Inc. Both are now subsidiaries of Dallas based Aventiv Technologies.
Shapiro, and his co-defendants David Schottenstein, identified by the Miami Herald as "members of one of America's richest families, and hedge fund manager, friend, and neighbor Kris Bortnovsky, used insider information to

profit from the stock market in two separate occasions. Profits for the JPay founder were $121,000, $600,000 for Schottenstein, and 3.5 million for Bortonovsky. This is what I call *trappin*, and a clear example of a *disproportionate share of wealth*. However, this is not the first time the whiff of corruption had tainted Shapiro's aura. He came under scrutiny by the New York department of corrections with JPay and Western Union services, both which bypassed stated procurement procedures. The contracts appear to violate New York's city law which restricts money transfer fees charged to prisoners and families to the maximum of $5.00 per transaction, while JPay service was charging $6.95 for transfer of $20 to $100, and Western Union services charged the same for transfer of $30-$75. [4] Rivera's family, my family, and millions of other families of the masses have all experienced these price gauging practices and tactics.

Power v. Poverty expounds on the many complexities of the Tennessee Department of Corrections and private prison Giant CCA formally known as corporate corrections of America, now known as Core Civic, pay to play schemes. Government officials, law makers, and lobbyists bend, twist, and turn the laws in favor of the highest bidder.

Power v. Poverty is a true, essential, uncomfortable, but much needed conversation that should be had with young black males before becoming another 1 in 3 statistic to enter these modern-day slave camps. There is no doubt that if young white males were incarcerated at the same rate as our young black males, it would be considered a national emergency.
While I have this opportunity, I'd like to applaud the efforts of the late great Mrs. Deborah Johnson of the Tennessee Department of Corrections (assassinated TDOC official), Senator Brenda Gilmore, who recently retired from her State Senate seat, and former Shelby County Judge Joe

Brown for all their many sacrifices by aiding and assisting our community.

-    Evan Knox #441566

FOREWORD BY J. TOWNE

I met Rivera L. Peoples through a beloved high school friend. Ten years later and she connected me to one of the largest purpose projects I've had to date. After meeting Peoples, he became "my peoples." I wanted to know more about his story, more about the logistics of his case, and most importantly, more about his mindset through this process.

This story is a riveting experience of a captivating journey as he unveils timeless truths about an ugly and all too familiar occurrence that black men have with the criminal justice system. I've written letters to prisoners for almost ten years, and I never thought I would read a more candid reality that American prison populations face every day. Likewise, I've seen the power of books that can cross cultural, socioeconomic, and geographical lines to communicate to diverse audiences. With this read, it is easy for me to determine how anyone, in any walk of life, could pick this book up and leave in awe while ready to put their hand to the plow and take part in the reformation work. This story depicts appalling truths while revealing the poverty that enables mass incarceration and the powers that sustain it. The story ends in a hopeful tune with a strategic path to the future of power.

Under my tutelage, I've celebrated with prisoners who have become a lot more things than the painful and confusing past that landed them in prison. I've celebrated with men who've become fathers and grandfathers, and I've celebrated with women who've walked through drug addiction and forgiveness. I've also celebrated with prisoners that have become authors. I'm more than elated to celebrate with Rivera as he walks his journey into becoming an author, but also into manhood. He has found his voice and purpose to advocate for those who look like him by exposing systemic issues that plague our nation.

He has positioned this book as a tool in the larger vision of the platform for advocacy that he's standing for, and that's beyond commendable. The world needs more people like him, and the world needs you to be informed and read this book.

Change is waiting for you.

Jennifer Towne, MA
Founder of Pens to Prison

INTRODUCTION

What comes to your mind when you hear, "Sentenced to life?" Do you imagine the judge hitting the gavel to seal the fate of a deserving individual? Do you automatically assume that person *must* be guilty to get that large of a sentence? Do you imagine some heinous criminal that deserves everything that he gets? Do you imagine this big, scary, black guy that everyone knows is a hopeless chance and was destined to a life of crime anyway? I don't know what comes to your mind or what stereotypes float in your psyche, but I have a truthful picture to paint of a system that funneled me through its dark reality.

I sat in trial court to hear those words, "Sentenced to life" plus 100 years. I wasn't destined to a life of crime. I wasn't some big, scary, black guy. I was 18 years old with a full life ahead of me.

Before you disregard this story as a woe-is-me saga, let's discuss the failures of the system that allowed this to be.

Justice system

Plainly stated, the law says that if a criminal defendant can't afford representation, they will be appointed an attorney by the court.

I was a poor 18-years-old inner-city kid with no guidance and direction. My mother was horribly addicted to crack cocaine. Trauma wreaked havoc early in my life as I watched my mother get shot in the chest at two years old. Domestic violence, neglect, and abandonment was a normal part of my upbringing because of this addiction. I vividly remember the screams and chaos in my home as my mother was carried away. We were all thinking she died. Although she lived through the fatal shot, her crack addiction did not die. She sold any and everything we had of value for her next hit. It was extremely embarrassing to witness everything we owned out on the street corner, and to come back to school after Christmas in the same clothes. My siblings and I hardly ever had a stable home. Six kids slept in motels and on couches of people that decided to be generous. Early on, my father was completely absent in my life. Going to school was not for learning, it was for safety. I had stabilization there in the form of meals, adults that seemingly cared, and a schedule that I could count on being the same, that is, on the days I made it to school. With no guidance, no resources to survive, no home to go to, and no skills to live by, all I had were friends that were underprivileged and impoverished like I was and looking to survive. I never wanted to be a criminal or associated with such societal rebellion, but I saw no other option.

My association with friends that committed crimes landed me in this deplorable predicament. I had no means or knowledge to navigate the situation I found myself in. Not only was I young and new to the world, but I was also still a child in mind and development. Everything about this newfound situation made me feel lost, powerless, and afraid. To add insult to injury, I was assigned a court-appointed attorney that scantily reviewed my case and never spoke with me before conducting my trial. At the time, I didn't know this was a breach of the law, but I still felt an inner urge to fight for myself. I chose to breach protocol and speak up during the trial about the attorney's failure to meet with me. I was given two options. I could sit there and be compliant with the attorney that was representing me (because who was this stranger? I never saw him before a day in my life) or I could sit in the back but, either way, the trial was proceeding with or without me.

Can you imagine sitting there listening to someone decide the direction of your life with full knowledge that they never consulted you about it? That wasn't the only sitting I've done. I was instructed to sit there quietly, powerless to stop any of it from happening, which led to me sitting in five different prisons having served 13 years of a sentence for a crime I did not commit.

During my time of bouncing to different prisons, I've had time to sit and reflect. I took a look around at all the people who were in there that looked like me with similar stories. I asked questions about why our stories were so similar. We grew up with moms and parents on drugs, we came from poverty-stricken, inner-city environments that were racked with crime, violence, and a struggle to meet basic resources. Not only were we poor, but we also experienced prison at an early age with hefty sentences.

None of this made sense on how we were alike; yet, there was nothing about this system that was making a difference. All these factors of hefty sentences, evasive and absent lawyers, inhumane prison conditions, with guard-to-inmate violence, and a continual disregard for our basic human rights made me dig deep inwardly. I had to take a long, hard reflective look at myself. I began with my personal history. Memories of my childhood experiences and the way I was shaped and developed to think about the world flooded my mind.

I recognized through all my life experiences filled with struggle, opposition, and defeat, that I was not this monstrously dangerous lowlife that needed to be unjustly locked up for a crime I didn't commit. I was a developing teenager that made a wrong choice in friends. I acknowledge that I was poor, without resources and lacked guidance, but that doesn't automatically mean that bad friends in a horrible situation means I deserve life in prison. I had to understand how this happened, and I longed to know what contributed to my being here. I wanted to know why there was so much likeness in the situations of those who are in with me and the circumstances surrounding our situations that brought us together for this demise.

I couldn't sleep. I had so many questions that didn't [initially] have answers. Amidst the sound of chaos and night terrors happening around me, I couldn't sleep with this burning desire to know why. I recognized that the similarities of the individuals around me had to be more than a coincidence. This was not a matter of chance, and I had to figure out what it meant.

Because of the injustices I experienced getting here, I turned my attention to the system at work. I wondered why no one seemed to care for the inner-city poor kid and allowed this to happen. I had to educate myself on the system, structure, and intended function of American prison systems. Interesting findings led me to discover a money trail that birthed this book.

My name is Rivera Peoples, and this is the first-hand account you've been waiting for. There are plenty of books and stories that discuss triumphs after prison, or theologically discuss the ideologies of what it is supposed to be. However, this book encompasses the real and raw truth of my current reality and exposes the system that permits this injustice.

I wrote this book for you. You have the power to stop funneling at-risk youth into the big business of prison profiteering. I want you to become aware of the problems that plague the system while lacking the functionality to prepare prisoners for re-entry to society. I want you to take a hard look at my story as a window into the dark reality that is prison culture. In this work, I unpack my personal journey for the trial of my life while unveiling the larger scheme of American history that has permitted systemic and systematic injustice to prevail over marginalized communities. From this has come a profitable mess called 'mass incarceration' that is fueled by injustice and inequity. I didn't know anything about this system at work until I found myself sentenced to a life in prison with a lot of time and a lot of questions.

I had a lot of questions, but I want you to have the answers. I want you to know the truth of the reality of millions of Americans that may or may not re-enter your community. Follow me as I lead you through the trial of my life, and we follow the money that unveils the scheme of America's mass incarceration.

Part I:
The Monster of Mass Incarceration

Rivera L. Peoples

CHAPTER 1:
WHAT IS MASS INCARCERATION?

"Mass incarceration is a symptom of a larger problem, which I call 'America-ism's'. Classism, racism, and capitalism are the driving forces behind our broken justice system."

In layman's terms, mass incarceration is the method by which the United States locked up a lot of people for felony offenses, or unjustly placed harsher sentences on lesser crimes. That leaves room to question, why would this happen?

Let's jump into a quick history lesson to understand how masses of people became incarcerated. The type of people who have historically been mass incarcerated have two attributes in common: they're black, they're poor, and they're poor and black.

The history

It is no secret that the United States leads the world in incarceration. According to the World Prison Brief, the United States incarcerates a larger share of its population than any other country.[1] Estimates suggest there are over two million people incarcerated in the United States[2], accounting for 20% of the world's incarcerated population[3]. Of the millions of individuals incarcerated, the vast majority are poor black males. According to the American Civil Liberties, there is an outstanding racial and economic difference in *who* is incarcerated. One in every three Black boys born in America can expect to go to prison compared to one in every 17 White boys and one in every six Latino boys.[4]

Tracing the history of how the United States' incarceration rates arrived to this point stems from a long history of legal policies and loopholes that unduly impacts black and poor communities. The first major loophole that constitutes (literally and metaphorically) this issue of mass incarceration is the clause in the 13th amendment of the Constitution that abolished slavery. The clause, 'except for punishment of crime,' created a harsh reality for many [Black] Americans. Not merely a year later, convict leasing began as a profitable business model for the exception within the amendment to become the rule of big business. States realized they could solve their issue of prison overcrowding by leasing their prisoners to industrialists and local planters that would pay the state for the prisoners' labor.[5] Buyers were responsible for housing and feeding prisoners, so while adding money to the state's budget, it eliminated their responsibility to house and feed prisoners.

Eventually, public outcry for the prisoners led to state's dismantling this practice and keeping prisoners' labor for public projects. They worked on what was deemed chain gangs.[6]

This notion of profiting from prisoners was only the beginning of what would lead to a system-wide American problem. President Reagan's establishment of the nation's war-on-drugs and tough-on-crime policies perpetuated this problem.[7] Simply said, those policies made it legal to disproportionately imprison black people. There is extensive documentation that lawmakers were clearly aware that the laws would have an overwhelmingly negative effect on black people, and continued forward with their institution.[8] Additionally, successive administrations have upheld and continued to add fuel to this wildfire.

We could rattle off the long history of facts for days on end, but two blaring statistics are crippling our society and exploiting a community of people -- that is, poor black people are incarcerated at significantly higher rates than any other demographic of people, and those invested in prisons profit from this terrible reality.

The Current State of Affairs

To date, 80 billion tax dollars are spent annually on the American criminal justice system.[9] There is widespread knowledge that crime in America is a costly expenditure for a system that does not work. Advocates and lobbyists are constantly calling to awareness that communities aren't safer because of policing or policing practices. Recidivism rates (in layman's terms, it's the likelihood that a prisoner will go back to prison after getting out. It's often referred to as reoffending) remains at an all-time high. According to the Bureau of Justice Statistics, a study conducted between 2012 and 2017 found that 71% of prisoners in 34 states returned to prison within five years.[10] Those numbers reflect the national average as a recent review of the data found the United States recidivism rate is 76.6% within five years, leading the world in rearrests.[11]

The Fair Fight Initiative lists 10 main (but not limited to) reasons that Mass Incarceration exists[12], those being:

- Exorbitant Bail – Nearly 500,000 people sit in prison at any given time, waiting for trial because they cannot afford to pay bail and be released to await trial. Research shows that people awaiting trial who are not in jail are less likely to be convicted and less likely to be imprisoned if they are convicted.

- Mandatory Minimum Sentencing – Laws that dictate minimum sentencing strip judges of the ability to account for individual circumstances.

- Three Strikes Laws –These laws mandate a sentence of 25 years to life after conviction for a third felony.

- "Truth" in Sentencing Laws – These laws mandate that people convicted of crimes must serve the majority of their sentences before becoming eligible for parole.

- The War on Drugs – It's been explicitly documented that policymakers understood the war on drugs would disproportionally affect people of color. Today, nearly 50 percent of incarcerated people in the federal system are in prison for drug offenses, and two-thirds of that population are people of color.

- Harsh Punishment for Non-Violent Crimes Resulting in Increased Plea Bargaining – As mandatory minimums became more commonplace, more and more people charged with crimes increasingly opt to plea to lesser charges that still include imprisonment, even when they are innocent, rather than face incredibly harsh punishments if they're convicted at trial.

- Problematic probation and parole – Strict rules regarding probation and parole cause many people to be sent back to prison for minor violations. Nearly

25 percent of state prison admissions are due to probation violations.

- Lack of Mental Health Services –A huge proportion of incarcerated people face mental health issues, approximately 1.2 million, according to Mental Health America. Prison guards, lacking training in responding to mental health crises, resort to use of force and solitary confinement – both known to aggravate mental health issues.

- Longer sentences and more life sentences – One in nine people currently incarcerated are serving a life sentence, with a third of those serving life without parole.

- Private prisons and profit motive – Private prisons and a vast number of private vendors are financially incentivized to maintain mass incarceration.

Let's not shy away from the systematic intentionality of this fact. Recall in the introduction I stated there was a trail laced with dollars and greed that I followed to make sense of all of this. This is where my reality comes in to play.

Federal Prisons vs. Private Prisons

The emergence of private prisons came about when Federal and state prisons experienced mass overcrowding. Beds for prisoners were limited and living conditions declined as the number of incarcerated individuals increased, but the beds for them did not. To "solve" this problem, the Corrections Corporation of America (CCA) was founded as the first and largest private prison company in 1983.[13]

Interestingly enough, one of the founders of CCA (now known as CoreCivic[14]) is from Tennessee, my home state. Discovering this fact made my quest to know more personal. CoreCivic has three primary founders, Tom Beasley, Doctor Crants, and T. Don Hutto.[15,16] These men banded together to remove the responsibility of prisons being handled and operated by the federal and state government, to incorporate a business model for prison reformation at a private state level. This is where the money trail begins, but I didn't understand the motive until I understood the men who were leading the way (we'll discuss this further in Chapter 3).

Here's what you need to know about private prisons: they don't work either. CoreCivic founders pride themselves as the solution to the failure of federal and state prisons' ability to constitutionally house inmates without violating their human rights. The facts are evident that federal and state prisons aren't upholding these basic principles, but private prisons don't display a significant difference in the health and welfare of prisoners. Nonetheless, there has been a gradual incline in the institution and placement of inmates in private prisons as compared to public facilities.

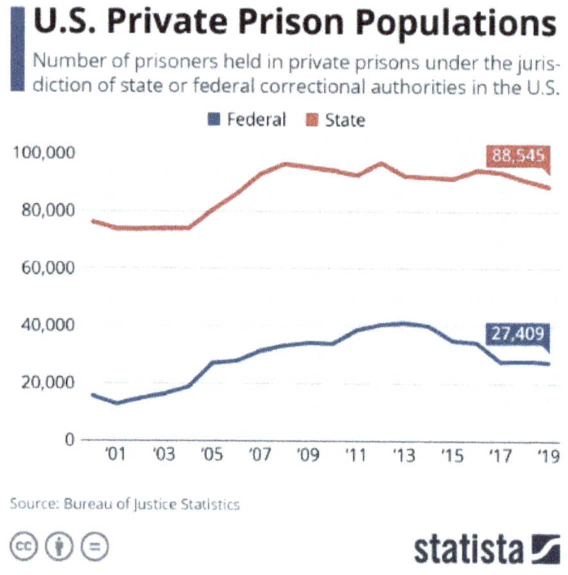

Private prisons are no walk in the park compared to federally funded prisons. Additionally, privatization isn't assisting the savings bottom line. Private prisons' average savings are about 1% compared to federally funded prisons, and that is achieved by cutting labor costs.[17] The lack of staffing, coupled with inhumane conditions, has a reverse effect on the inmates as it propagates more violence and unrest, leading to penalties and delayed releases.

Dr. Galinato of Washington State University led a study that explored the privatization of prisons and the effects on incarceration rates. The study found private prisons increased average incarceration rates by 178 new prisoners per population of one million per year. This increase costs states roughly $1.9 million to $10.6 million per year if those inmates are housed in private prisons. Moreover, the bottom line increases as well as the effect of total new incarcerations and sentencing length based on private prison beds per capita, guilty verdicts for select crimes, and the likelihood of individual incarceration in corrupt states.[19]

Essentially, private prisons were set in place to be a more effective alternative to the costly, ineffective approach of publicly funded prisons but, in fact, findings suggest private prisons "operate much the same as public facilities," and due to the need to save on resources, they underperform compared to federal facilities.[20, 21]

If you think the statistics are not enough, let's lean into the facts from this Twitter discussion. Dallas Liam tweets a potential path to financial gain from prison profiteering. Although his credibility could not be verified (definitely a troll), his tweet went viral as the reality of the numbers reveal a daunting, and rather easy, path to quick financial success based on prisoners. The series of tweets are as follows:

"Owning a private prison gives an investor a recurring and predictable stream of high margin revenue. The government contracts are long-term in nature and very lucrative. I have managed to make over $35,000 per prisoner annually. Let's breakdown a deal.

I've owned and operated private prisons for over two decades. Private prisons are the single greatest real estate investment vehicle around. Here is what I have learned. I have purchased the Eagle Nest Facility in 2008. Total cost was $30 million with 25% down ($7.5 million). The facility has 1,200 beds implying a cost per bed of only $25,000 (building a new prison is in excess of $150k per bed). I entered a perpetual contract with the United States Marshall Services at $20 million per year with 5% escalators per year. In the first year, we generated $5 million in free cash flow, a 67% cash on cash return.

Prison owners get paid per person. The more people, the more money. Here are the economics per person:

- $100/day per person in revenues
- $25/day per person in fixed variable cost
- $35/day per person in fixed costs
- $40/day per person in straight margin

To increase my cash flow, I spent a significant amount of money on lobbying efforts to win a judge who was hard on crime. This paid off by the end of year two. To pay me back, the judge sent most young men (higher margin than older men) to my facility. Cash flow went up 3x. By year four, cash flows were $15 million at 95% occupancy. To maximize my investment, I started to market the facility to outside investors. Halfway through year four, we sold the facility to private equity for 10x cash flow or $150 million.

In four years, I turned $7.5 million into a clean $150 million. I took this money and reinvested it into other prisons across southern states. Today, I manage an investment portfolio of over $1.5 billion in prison real estate.

Tips:

- Get financing from individual investors
- Focus on states "hard on crime"
- Prisoners = money. You need crime to profit
- You can use prisoners to generate ancillary revenues at dirt cheap wages (incredibly high margin)
- Become best friends with judges

To date, the current administration under President Joe R. Biden has signed an executive order that will not renew contracts with private prisons to eliminate the incentivization to incarcerate.[22]

To bring matters to my home state, the Tennessee legislature just recently passed another 'Tough on Crime Sentencing' bill that increases the amount of time that inmates spend in prison. House speaker Cameron Sexton, who largely supports the initiative stated that he's, "not opposed to criminal justice reform - including to prevent crimes before anyone ends up in prison, but that's another conversation for another year."[23]

Despite what's happening in my home state, the executive order may appear to be a step in the correct direction. Only six institutions will be impacted by the order without a clear plan of action, but there's more to the story. What happens to privately funded prisons that are not federally contracted? Further, what happens to the estimated 14,000 inmates who are currently in those prisons? Will they now be forced to relocate to another private facility and be subjected to overcrowding, understaffing, and worse inhumane conditions?

Although I respect and appreciate the [potential] turn of events, I have been to five prisons during my time incarcerated. Decision-makers, lawmakers, and activists alike won't know the severity of this issue until they walk these cold, dark corridors and hear the clanging of chains and prison bars, along with the screams of individuals losing their minds while trying to remain sane. Again, I understand prison is not supposed to be a sunny-meadow walk-in-the-park but permitting an environment that is a bottomless pit of endless suffering and corruption that epically fails to rehabilitate the person from that environment is no way serving justice to the community that inmates will return to. Power leaders and bottom-line signers of America will not understand the urgency to transform this money hungry system unless they become one of the masses.

CHAPTER 2:
ONE OF THE MASSES

"We have a system of justice in [the US] that treats you much better if you're rich and guilty than if you're poot and innocent."
- Bryan Stevenson

Almost 15 years into a life-plus sentence at five different prisons that give hell on earth a physical address, I hate to say it, but I'm one of the masses that wakes up to this nightmare every day. There are many books that can babble facts about what it's like to be a victim of the inhumane and unjust system that produces mass incarceration, but the reality of my lived experiences is almost surreal.

I was wrongfully convicted of first-degree murder and received a sentence of life with the possibility of parole after 51 years, plus 100 years for robbery and kidnapping. I was prosecuted and convicted of being criminally responsible for the conduct of another person. You read that correctly - criminally *responsible* for the conduct of another person *after* not receiving a fair trial. My plight with the unjust system began at Northwest Correctional Facility.

Northwest Correctional Facility - Inmate #475644

In September of 2010, I entered Northwest Correctional Complex located in Tiptonville, Lake County, Tennessee. I was a child that had no awareness of the journey I was about to step into, but I knew I had to protect myself. I was so eager to prove myself that my immaturity showed in my actions and my decisions.

I became quickly aware of how vile and evil this prison was. The floor was often cold and wet, the food was often unidentifiable, and the smell was consistently beyond repulsive. To make matters worse, the officers were corrupt and proud about it. The prison staff enjoyed abusing their power, and the lack of accountability they had is what cultivated the danger, breaches, and violations of the law, along with the inhumane oppression and degradation of inmates. They would often state, "The only difference between you and me is that you got caught." They were often braggadocious and similarly belittling. I saw and experienced female prison staff regularly and often have sex with inmates. I witnessed inmates gain access to drugs and other supposedly illegal contraband. I watched gangs jump and kill other inmates while prison staff covered homicide murders with legal jargon and falsification. Because of all the turmoil around me, mixed with my need for protection and safety, I became a product of this "Thunder Dome" environment. My involvement in a gang riot led me to my next destination.

Morgan County Correctional Complex - Inmate #475644

Morgan county is a medium security prison that holds 120 beds for maximum security. One of those beds was mine for a year and a half. I was placed in solitary confinement where I spent 23 hours of each day behind a solid steel door. My food was pushed through a tray compartment in the door, so I rarely saw or heard from anyone. The one hour of recreation I was given was only enough time to recover from the underground hole I was brought from. It was enough of a reminder that a world beyond the walls did exist, and I couldn't lose sight of that. That simple task became the most challenging part of my life.

The severity of this style of punishment isn't in being isolated. The grimness of solitary confinement is found in the loud screams of quiet and the raging thoughts of torment that become your company. The silence was deafening all around me, and for the first time in my life, there was nothing. No family to struggle with, no friends to hang out with, no classmates to get by in class with, no cellmates to reminisce with. Nothing. No laughter, ruthless banter, arguing, buzzer sounds of prison locks, fights to break out...nothing. There were no decisions to make. There were no familiar or unfamiliar faces to engage with. There were no altercations happening around me to make the day go by faster. There was no warm mail from loved ones to circulate my mind with their thoughts. The essence of 'nothing' manifested fully as I sat for agonizing hours with nothing. A war broke out in my mind between what I used to know as reality and what I was facing as my current predicament. Although it is deemed solitary confinement, my mind tried, with every moment, for several days on end, to break out of the box that had me bound. Each day, I teetered the line of sanity and insanity as I grappled with the monstrous facts of my existence. It was the lowest time of my life. I eventually learned to expect that no one was coming for me. No one would get me out of the box I found myself in, so I had to figure out a way. I overcame many days in solitude by channeling my focus on a way to get out of the box. It wasn't until I was alone through those days that I recognized my freedom was confined inside a much larger box (at which I now know as mass incarceration). I learned that the real battle I was coming up against would be the battle of my life. I felt my time in confinement was development, and cruel and unusual training for the giants I had ahead.

I mustered the mental fortitude to remain on the side of sanity long enough to develop, mature, and make it to my next prison.

West Tennessee State Penitentiary - Inmate #475644

West Tennessee State Penitentiary was in the middle of my prison quests. Newly off solitary confinement, I had a renewed sense of gratitude, as well as lots of focus. Despite the magnitude of the corruption around me, I wanted to fill my mind with more about the world outside prison walls. I made it my mission to learn more about economics. I firmly believed that "money makes the world go 'round" and, during my time there, I committed to learning more about economics. I knew that I needed an attorney, and that representation was the only way I could give myself a fighting chance at coming against an entire system that was designed for me to be a part of it. During my time of serving at West Tennessee State, I became laser-focused on getting my case overturned. I became obsessed with learning more about and gaining money to help my fight to freedom. Although I spent 18 months at Morgan County, I was only at West Tennessee State for a year until I made it to my next destination - Turney Center Industrial Complex.

Turney Center Industrial Complex - Inmate #475644

I quickly learned that prisons were not what they marketed themselves to be to the public. Guards were proud of their criminal activity along with the black market of prison that floated contraband and commissary around to increase the drug use, violence, and homicide that occurred. Every prison I encountered had its fair share of corruption stemming from the head of command down to the inmates themselves, but Turney Center was slightly different. I don't give them the award for being the "best" prison necessarily, but compared to my other stays, Turney Center was strictly by-the-book on the rules. This prison operated on the order set, and everyone knew that the rules were the standard. There wasn't *as* much pride, ego, humiliation, or abusive force that "runs the yard." Because there weren't as many traumatic events happening around me, it allowed me to act on the focus I carried to the facility. At Turney, education became key to unlocking the scheme that led to mass incarceration in America.

I was accepted to and received the opportunity to join a program called T.H.E.I. The Tennessee Higher Education Initiative has the mission of providing support to incarcerated scholars as they pursue college degrees. T.H.E.I. had a joint mission of preparing prisoners for release and re-entry. This program was eye-opening and dynamic for my development. It offered me the opportunity to learn about American history, law, and government in ways I had never known. My time with the program was extremely impactful in teaching me how power operates in our country and what was most important to American society - the dollars on the bottom line.

I thank God for allowing me to experience a college atmosphere-style of learning while in prison. I had a very influential professor, Dr. Benson, who made learning a fun and engaging activity, which is something I never experienced before. Dr. Benson was the coolest teacher I ever had. I deeply connected with his humorously sarcastic style of presenting knowledge. I don't think it was ironic that he was Canadian and had such an educated opinion on the American government. Dr. Benson's personality made me want to sit at his feet and soak up all of his knowledge while also wanting to go sit at a bar with him as a good friend. He left such an impression on me as a person because of the knowledge he imparted to me along with the desire to know more.

One of the most influential facts I learned from Dr. Benson, relative to the American government, was that representation was for the rich and wealthy of the country *first* (this is the beginning of privilege and will be discussed in later chapters). The light bulb clicked for me in these series of classes on how governmental influences, specifically money-hungry agendas, were voted on and placed into law. It all began to make sense as my hunger to know more grew deeper.

I owe Dr. Benson and the T.H.E.I. program many thanks. I firmly believe a program like this belongs inside of every prison. Although I wasn't able to finish the program, my quest to self-educate and grow did not stop there. I moved on to another prison and moved deeper in my newfound love to "know."

Trousdale Turner Correctional facility

Trousdale. Trousdale. Trousdale. This section in this chapter underscores the barbaric fate of those who are caged here. This prison is nicknamed "Belly of the Beast," and rightfully so, as it's the worst prison in the state of Tennessee. In this regard, "worst" is not solely my opinion, but the facts concerning the number of homicides, suicides, and assaults, along with inhumane conditions and abusive treatment, reflect the facts of my experiences here. All the corruption from other prisons pale in comparison to the travesty that comprises this facility. I left Turney Center so excited to learn more and liberate myself in a rehabilitative environment, but I had no idea what I was walking into. The corruption is God-forsaken. The only plausible solution for this facility is to transfer everyone to another facility and burn it to the ground, never to look back.

I have seen things done to humans that should never be a thought in the heart and mind of another person. I have witnessed the blatant disregard for serious medical needs, resulting in the death of inmates. I've watched countless inmates from this facility die without their family knowing until days later, and the persistent flow of reports and complaints from this facility reflect the arrogant neglect. Inmates have been locked down for weeks without food and showers, while the prison lacked staffing. In addition to other tragedies that regularly take place here, my cell has been utterly trashed and destroyed with no just cause, along with the humiliating and jeering insults from the prison staff practicing dominance. As of late, I have requested medical treatment for a lump in my shoulder. It began about the size of a golf ball and has since doubled in size. I have continued to request medical attention and have yet to receive any attention.

It did not take me long to understand who the beast was and why this facility was considered the belly. There is no doubt in my mind that this prison reflects the overall bestial nature of mass incarceration, ya' know, the morally despicable and inherently decrepit system that has continued for far too long. This facility is considered the belly of the beast because inmates are sent here to be consumed by the beast. The belly is responsible for consumption and processing with the only product to be returned as an output is waste. There shouldn't be any question as to why the death count is so high, the psychological disorders are ignored and outrageously increasing, all while the silence from facility officials is so loud. As CoreCivic reports, "No one dies at the facility" but the insurmountable truth is, if the belly does its job, everyone is consumed - one way or another.

Many advocates and activists only campaign for buzzwords like "physical abuse," "violence," "mental health," and "treatment disparities" of prison conditions. All of those campaigns are important and rightfully need public attention. However, here at Trousdale, I have witnessed the latent oppression that goes beyond 'cruel and unusual' and advances to 'gross and dark' evil. It is the snide, underlying agenda to intentionally dehumanize us, one rule and one show of force at a time. For instance, using the bathroom is a natural part of being human, right? Being that the toilet is in the cell with us, all my former prison stays required us to 'Drop and flush.' This means, as soon as poop drops, we flush. It's a small gesture that goes a long way in keeping the facility livable for all. Not only is it a courtesy to our cell mate, but it's a courtesy to everyone else as the smell of fecal matter doesn't stay confined to the cell. Trousdale does this differently. We are limited to two flushes per hour. Can you imagine being placed in a cell or on a cell block where fully grown men have to allow their feces to sit because they have used all of their flushes-per-hour? Can you imagine the smell? Can you imagine the anger and disgust that comes with being forced to smell the foul odor? Can you imagine this happening to more than one group of cellmates, compounding the smell and animosity within the facility? I hope you're envisioning the animalistic nature of being confined in a cage to sit with its waste.

Now that you've imagined the impact that this seemingly minor rule has on everyone involved, imagine the compounding magnitude of all their rules working together in a dehumanizing effort. Trousdale taught me about the lack of accountability coupled with the privacy that breeds mistreatment from this CoreCivic facility; except, it is more than a notion that mistreatment goes beyond humane conditions to a direct outcome of dehumanization. In my experience, the one thing that makes Trousdale the worst prison in the state of Tennessee is the known fact that doing time at Trousdale is not a life sentence, but a death sentence. However, I refuse to die in any way, shape, form, or fashion.

At the time of this publication, I am serving time at Trousdale with my case in review.

Other Inmates 101

I've done a lot of time behind bars. Enough time to know that my experiences aren't isolated incidents. Accidents can be excused, mistakes sometimes happen, but when the same things happen to the same types of people, a system is doing what it was originally created to do. That is the foundation of this problem, and the solutions will be discussed in later chapters, but I think this section would be incomplete if I only focused on my experiences.

I have quickly learned I am not alone in being one of the masses. All of these issues impact us differently. Medically, I have watched an elderly black man die from a lack of medical attention. He had a large tumor on his stomach that went uncared for while being forced to eat prison food that went against his diet restrictions. Medically, I've watched an elderly white man pass out and be ignored for so long that his medical situation was beyond rescue. I watched the ambulance come and act as if they were reviving him, but we all knew the truth of his fate. That wasn't the only time a lack of supervision has resulted in major problems. We have been left alone for hours without any guard or supervisor on command. Over 100 inmates across three housing units completely left to themselves is problematic on a good day. We had the ability to do *whatever* we so desired. Can you imagine the awful limitless possibilities of what could happen in the state's largest prison with some of its greatest offenders that have no supervision over an extended period of time? That's not a day I wanted to be here either, or a reality I ever thought that I would witness in prison.

THE TENNESSEAN

NEWS

CoreCivic to settle shareholders lawsuit for $56 million

TRAVIS LOLLER Associated Press

Published 11:29 a.m. CT April 20, 2021

Show image info ˅

NASHVILLE — CoreCivic says it will pay $56 million to settle a lawsuit by shareholders who accused the private prison operator of inflating its stock prices by misrepresenting the quality and value of its services.

Question for those who know better: Is there some reason why the State of Tennessee being a large institutional shareholder of @CoreCivic at the same time that it's supposed to be regulating the company's many prisons in this State *wouldn't* present a conflict of interest?

Defense Attorney Horwitz of Nashville takes to Twitter to depict invested interest the State of Tennessee has with Core Civic. He was ordered by the U.S Magistrate Judge Jeffery Frensley to delete this tweet among others. [2]

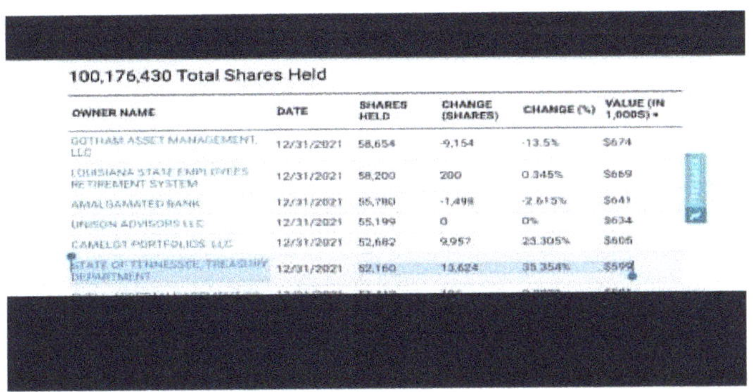

100,176,430 Total Shares Held

OWNER NAME	DATE	SHARES HELD	CHANGE (SHARES)	CHANGE (%)	VALUE (IN 1,000S) *
GOTHAM ASSET MANAGEMENT, LLC	12/31/2021	58,654	-9,154	-13.5%	$674
LOUISIANA STATE EMPLOYEES RETIREMENT SYSTEM	12/31/2021	58,200	200	0.345%	$669
AMALGAMATED BANK	12/31/2021	55,780	-1,498	-2.615%	$641
UNISON ADVISORS LLC	12/31/2021	55,199	0	0%	$634
CAMELOT PORTFOLIOS LLC	12/31/2021	52,682	9,957	23.305%	$605
STATE OF TENNESSEE, TREASURY DEPARTMENT	12/31/2021	52,160	13,624	35.354%	$599

According to the NASDAQ, Core Civic has 121 million shares held by stockholders making the value of those shares will over 1 billion shares. [3]

CXW Institutional Holdings

Ownership Summary

Institutional Ownership	82.54 %
Total Shares Outstanding (millions)	121
Total Value of Holdings (millions)	$1,151

Of the 100,176,430 shares Core Civic has, the State of Tennessee holds 52,160 shares. [4]

Today, Tennessee's incarceration rates stand out internationally

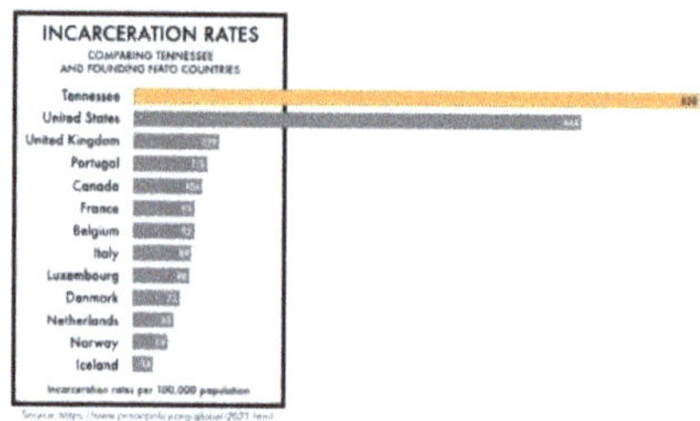

In the U.S., incarceration extends beyond prisons and local jails to include other systems of confinement. The U.S. and state incarceration rates in this graph include people held by these other parts of the justice system, so they may be slightly higher than the commonly reported incarceration rates that only include prisons and jails. Details on the data are available in States of Incarceration: The Global Context. We also have a

A comparison for the rate of incarceration for the state of Tennessee prisons as compared to founding nations per 100,000 population. [5]

People of color are overrepresented in
prisons and jails

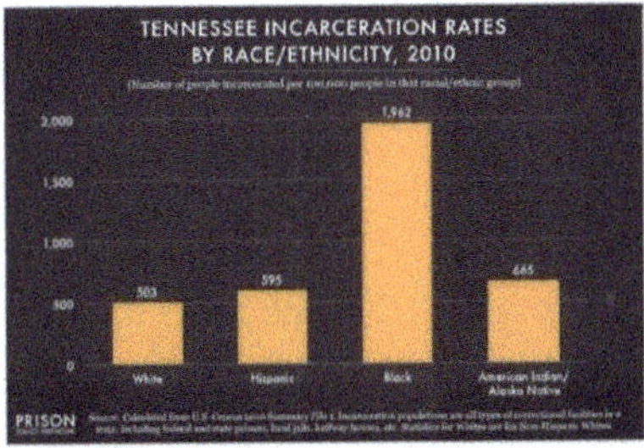

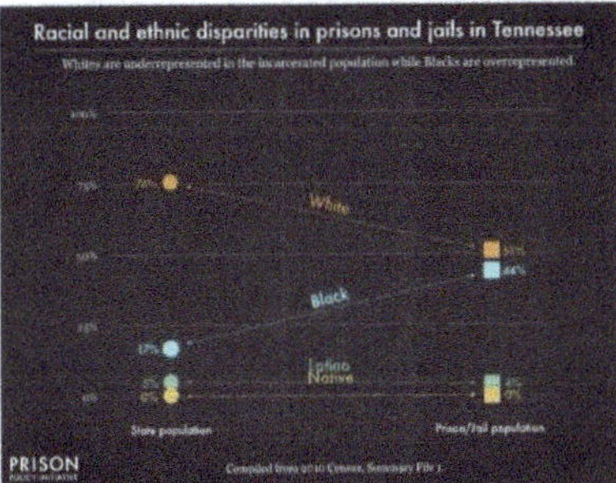

*The Prison Policy Initiative depicts the racial disparities for incarceration rates in
the state of Tennessee. The rate of incarceration for African American largely out
numbers any other racial group.*[6]

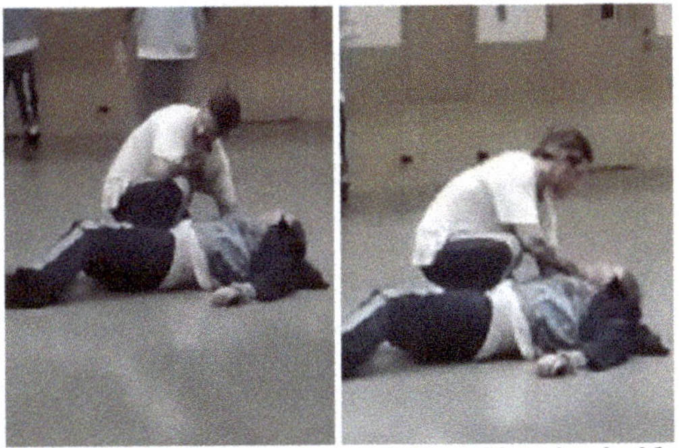

*Yet another unresponsive inmate at an undisclosed location inside a Core
Civic Facility.* [7]

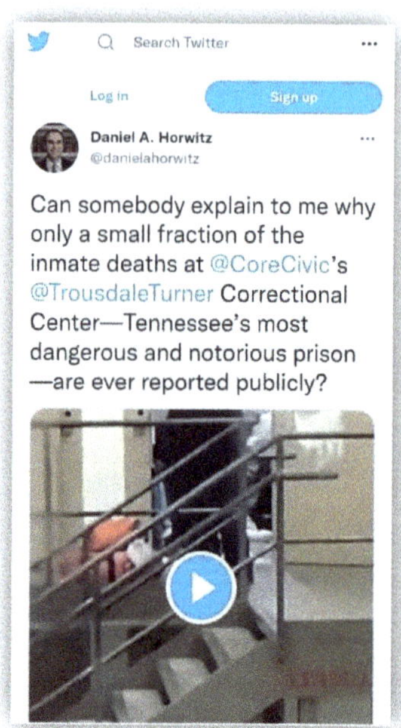
Search Twitter
Log in
Sign up
Daniel A. Horwitz
@danielahorwitz
Can somebody explain to me why only a small fraction of the inmate deaths at @CoreCivic's @TrousdaleTurner Correctional Center—Tennessee's most dangerous and notorious prison—are ever reported publicly?

← Tweet
Daniel A. Horwitz
@danielahorwitz
CoreCivic: (1) lets people get murdered in its prisons, (2) on video, then (3) withholds the videos based on claims that their release would compromise security, which (4) CoreCivic itself compromises by chronically understaffing its prisons. Incredible.

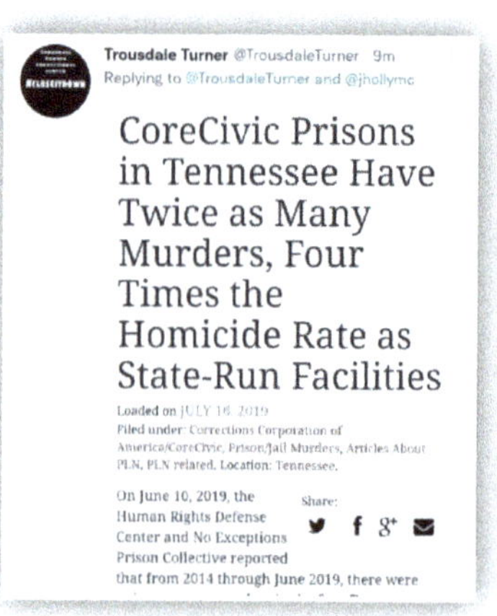
Trousdale Turner @TrousdaleTurner 9m
Replying to @TrousdaleTurner and @jhollymc

CoreCivic Prisons in Tennessee Have Twice as Many Murders, Four Times the Homicide Rate as State-Run Facilities

Loaded on JULY 16, 2019
Filed under: Corrections Corporation of America/CoreCivic, Prison/Jail Murders, Articles About PLN, PLN related. Location: Tennessee.

On June 10, 2019, the Human Rights Defense Center and No Exceptions Prison Collective reported that from 2014 through June 2019, there were

Share:

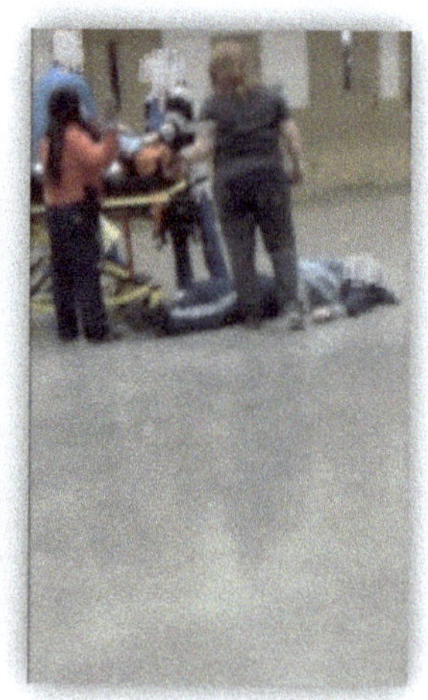

RIVERA L. PEOPLES

Down's post

Trousdale Turner - Close It Down
1d ·

7/21/22

RE: DEATH OF JOSHUA MINCE-DIES
YESTERDAY IN CORECIVIC'S TTCC

https://www.gofundme.com/f/funeral-funds-
for-joshua-lynn-mince-dies

Family is still looking for information. Joshua
Mince-Dies was housed in Bravo Bravo pod, the
same place a man was thrown off top tier last
week and 3 were flown to Vanderbilt.

"My brother was holding property for the person
thrown from top tier (until he was able to get
them back). I'm only telling you these things in
hopes we can pull this information together and
try to understand.

"I know he was stabbed a few weeks ago in the
eye. They refused him medical care."

*Image of Joshua Mince Dies saving the life of another inmate inside a Core Civic
facility, unfortunately weeks later no one would be there to help save Joshua life.*

9

Death at Trousdale 12/2/21
Family Looking For Answers

We just received two messages from family regarding a death at TTCC yesterday.

"My child father died yesterday we need answers, his child, family and I need real answers other than he was sick and we can't view his body. They told us they'll bury him without us viewing his body they said the only way we can view his body is if we cremate him and I honestly think they're trying to cover up what they've done to him."

"My child who is 5 father died in their care. We need true answers. How can you deny a man medical treatment? Why would you put a sick man in the hole by himself to die? My child has to live the rest of his life without his father. I'm hurt mad angry sad and frustrated but I need answers now."

Many of you have unfortunately been through this already and they need all

Family members looking for answers to loved one's death.[10]

2021 Inmate Deaths In Custody

	Date	Facility	Name	Age	Sex	ID	Cause
1	1/1/21	MCCX	Knight, Brian	45	M	560527	Natural-Illness
2	1/4/21	TTCC	Hall, Randall	49	M	130432	Accidental-Inadvertent
3	1/5/21	NWCX	Boin, Scotty	61	M	456486	Suicide
4	1/7/21	TCIX	Kilburn, Billy	56	M	722280	Natural-Illness
5	1/7/21	HMSI	Henning, Vale	32	M	429484	Natural-Illness
6	1/11/21	HCCF	Seay, Antonio	40	M	374485	Accidental-Inadvertent
7	1/11/21	NECX	Hodges, Chad	40	M	328965	Accidental-Inadvertent
8	1/12/21	NECX	Muñoz, Marquis	28	M	613064	Accidental-Inadvertent
9	1/14/21	TCIX	Pyburn, Marty	62	M	144084	Natural-Illness
10	1/15/21	TTCC	Chandler, Mickey	71	M	560626	Natural-Illness
11	1/16/21	MCCX	Johnson, Jordan	27	M	527086	Accidental-Inadvertent
12	1/16/21	SCCX	Bean, William	66	M	599040	Natural-Illness
13	1/16/21	SCCF	Hart, Randy	58	M	531924	Natural-Illness
14	1/17/21	NECX	Bias, Warner	81	M	411095	Natural-Illness
15	1/18/21	NWCX	Gerber, Craig	49	M	520810	Natural-Illness
16	1/19/21	MCCX	McClain, Jake	65	M	218249	Natural-Illness
17	1/20/21	MCCX	Miller, Brandon	28	M	515059	Accidental-Inadvertent
18	1/21/21	TTCC	Person, Ivy	64	M	121766	Natural-Illness
19	1/24/21	MCCX	Mitchell, Charles	79	M	288173	Natural-Illness
20	1/24/21	WTRC	Jackson, Antonina	20	F	613846	Pending
21	1/25/21	NWCX	Stewart, Roger	41	M	309210	Accidental-Inadvertent
22	1/27/21	NECX	Burton, Devedrick	33	M	424141	Suicide
23	1/28/21	NCCX	Burnette, Benjamin	37	M	617230	Natural-Illness
24	1/28/21	NWCX	Taylor, Tommy	59	M	426670	Natural-Illness
25	1/30/21	DSNF	Hollnsworth, Duncan	64	M	474991	Natural-Illness
26	1/31/21	NWCX	Hutcheson, Jack	66	M	612735	Natural-Illness
27	2/1/21	MCCX	Butler, Eric	48	M	422445	Suicide
28	2/6/21	NECX	Compton, Gratin	58	M	106666	Natural-Illness
29	2/6/21	HMSI	Eggleston, Frances	23	M	603660	Accidental-Inadvertent
30	2/7/21	NECX	Crittenden, Jarrod	29	M	484734	Homicide
31	2/13/21	SCCF	Laguire, Robert	68	M	536601	Natural-Illness
32	2/15/21	WCFA	Oates, Chico	35	M	361101	Suicide
33	2/19/21	DSNF	Hobbs, Clyde	72	M	119137	Natural-Illness
34	2/23/21	NWCX	Jackson, Oleary	65	M	147746	Natural-Illness
35	2/24/21	TTCC	Childress, Terry	37	M	623865	Homicide
36	2/26/21	DSNF	Biggers, Tony	61	M	425122	Natural-Illness
37	3/6/21	TTCC	Kirkwood, Kenneth	41	M	242497	Accidental-Inadvertent

The following images are pictures of Mr. Ivy Person #121766. Mr. Person is one of many inmates that have medical conditions that necessitate regular medical attention. Mr. Person had an enlarged tumor in his stomach that ultimately led to his death. Instead of adequate medical attention, he was isolated to a cell by himself, unattended by any prison personnel, for critical time leading up to his final days. May he rest in peace, but not in vain. We know that Mr. Person did not die of natural illnesses. He was neglected, leading to his death. However, the official report shows otherwise. He is unfortunately one of many examples.[11]

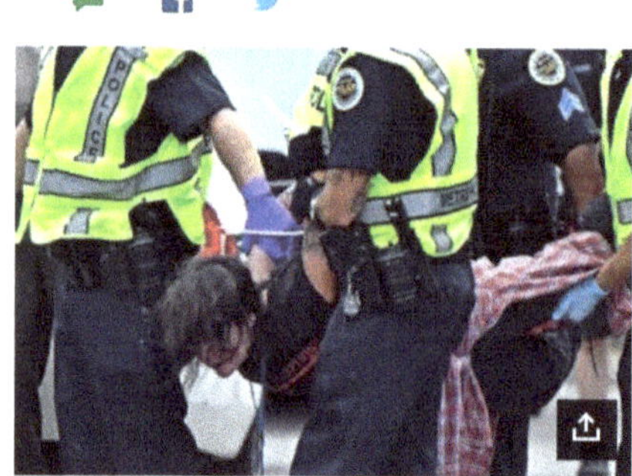

43 PHOTOS

3:44 p.m. CDT Aug. 6, 2018

Jeannie Alexander is carried off after being arrested with other protesters blocking the entrances of Nashville-based CoreCivic, the nation's largest owner and operator of private prisons, Monday Aug. 6, 2018, in Nashville, Tenn.

LARRY MCCORMACK / THE TENNESSEAN

How unjust and corrupt must a system be for someone to risk their own freedoms to protest for another human beings' rights. [12]

Unsanitary living conditions in Core Civic during the pandemic. Dirty laundry is left for a week leaving most inmates without a change of clothes. [13]

What a cell looks like after a typical shake down. Notice the destruction of the personal property with a complete abandonment of morality. No contraband was found.[14]

If the belly does its job, then everything it consumes is returned as waste.[15]

The list of concrete issues inside prison walls goes on and varies from person to person. There's a deeper issue lurking in these prison corridors as well. I didn't have to look far, and I didn't have to search at all because it was glaringly apparent that young black men were incarcerated at much higher rates than any other race. The vast majority, and I do mean 95% as generous, of young black men I encountered committed crimes of poverty and survival that landed them hefty fines and even heftier sentences. On the contrary to young black men, many of the old white men committed crimes of perversion accompanied with lighter sentences. This is no place to argue that the guy who inappropriately touched little children should receive a greater/lesser sentence than the guy who put drugs on the street. Here, I want to highlight intent and motive as compared to a system that distinguishes by race and economic status. The young black boy who was impoverished with no education got tired of the failure of government aid to provide for he and his family's needs, so illegal activity became a means of survival. Every day, I wake up to these lifeless prison walls and I see young black men wake up to the same fate (that I share in) for this very reason. To add, I've watched sexually heinous criminals spend six months here for utterly destroying the mental, emotional, and psychological future of their victims and brag about how their money and power will free them to go back and do the same things to the same or new victims. I found the difference to be money. Poor black boys that commit crimes of poverty with no education and a lack of proper governmental representation are trapped in a system designed to profit off their presence in prison.

Meanwhile, wealthy offenders with power and proper representation that commit crimes with full knowledge of their intentions, execution, and plan of escape through power and money are evading the full length of their consequences.

In essence, being one of the masses has very well meant a distinction between the haves and the have-nots that are ostracized from society. I have witnessed a stark difference in those that are here that never *wanted* to sell drugs to that neighborhood junkie and those that are here with no remorse for their sin against mankind. They pompously brag with full expectation to use their race, money, and power to become better at creating victims of prey on their release. My experiences witnessing this phenomenon day in and day out have awakened a desire for me to do something about what's happening here in America.

Let this be the record that states I will not become a beast while being in the belly. Let this serve as the record that neither my mind nor my body will be consumed by my most recent experiences. If I can endure solitary confinement, along with the open and acceptable corruption from authoritarians in a system designed to consume and make waste of me, then I will withstand to my last breath. When the judge hit the gavel that gave me my sentence, I expected hard. I expected long. I expected nightmares. I can honestly say that I never expected to be in the belly of the beast, and I never expected the suffocation of impossible. But each day I rise to persevere so that one less poor black boy will be in my position. I firmly believe my story was written before I was born, and I'm here to live each and every day to fulfill this newfound mission. It is simultaneously unsettling and reassuring.

CHAPTER 3: THE SCHEME REVEALED

"One prisoner wrote in his memoir that, as soon as the prison was privatized, his jailers "laid aside all objects of reformation and re-instated the most cruel tyranny, to eke out the dollar and cents of human misery."

To this point, I've alluded to the American dollar that makes this all possible. I've come to learn that there is much more to the scheme than the American dollar. However, money is the power engine that keeps legislation, crooked leaders, buyout lawmakers, and lobbyists in the big business of prison as an industry, and not its intended purpose. I didn't understand the motive until I understood the men who were leading the way. As you know, I'm housed in the state of Tennessee. I've been in state prisons, with my most recent experiences being housed at private prisons. This is important because more than being my home state, Tennessee is where the business of prison profiteering began.

Recall the brief mention of the founders of CoreCivic, Tom Beasley, Doctor Crants, and Don Hutto. It didn't make sense to me how these three worked together and were able to make a business model of America's inmates. I began to search individually into each of their backgrounds and exposed the systematic and systemic practices that lead to this billion-dollar giant.

At the time of conception, Tom Beasley was Chairman of the Tennessee Republican party and tasked with responsibility of selecting a new state corrections officer.[1] Instead of fulfilling his political obligation, he went on to view a vulnerable population that was plagued with systemic issues as an opportunity for economic gain. Beasley's political connections along with his business mind gave him the opportunity to "solve the prison problem and make a lot of money at the same time." [2] I now know by my experiences and the facts surrounding incarceration in these facilities that his mission has epically failed and instead it is to, 'Solve his money problem and make a lot of prison problems at the same time.'

One of the prominent political connections that gave him permission to begin the privatization of prisons in the state of Tennessee was his close friend, Lamar Alexander. Lamar Alexander was a Vanderbilt graduate who was the governor of the state of Tennessee from January 17, 1979 until January 17, 1987.[3] Could we say it's a coincidence that this was the exact time that Beasley wanted to push the agenda for the business of prison? Absolutely not, as former Governor Alexander assumed his office early as the state of Tennessee was receiving national outcry for the issues surrounding pardons granted by Governor Blanton.[4] Tennessee has a problematic history with issues regarding incarceration, and Beasley's money-making agenda only magnified the issue. As if it weren't enough that the Governor partnered with Beasley to make his financial dreams come true, he believed so much in the vision that he was persuaded to reap the benefits as well. It is widely known that his Honey, (yes, his wife's name is Honey Alexander) was one of the first investors in what was then Corporate Corrections of America. Governor Alexander played a critical role in lending his political power to provide permission for the beginning of prison profiteering.

Greed has a way of not caring who it negatively impacts, and long after Governor Alexander was out of office, Beasley and his team were well beyond start-up ventures as they placed a bid to buy-out all of the prisons in the state of Tennessee.[5] I find it so interesting that the bill to privatize all of the prisons in the state of Tennessee was withdrawn because those advocating for its passing were all business partners.[6,7] Yet, it's totally acceptable for this same industry to continue profiteering with the general acceptance of money over morality. What changed, Tennessee? What changed, America? Are the hearts and minds of our nation's leaders so depraved that we value economics over ethics?

The records show that money was at the root of this evil with more money certainly being the motive. Media focused on the relationship of private prison companies and Tennessee politicians to discover that Doctor Crants was the largest sole giver to lawmakers during the time that the Prison Privatization Bill was up for vote. Campaign finance records report he gave well over $100,000 over a two-year span to 84 legislative candidates.[8] Unfortunately, that's only what's known of his giving. Again, Doctor Crants was one of CoreCivic's leading founders. He was surely interested in seeing his investment give a return.

Doctor Crants certainly brought an interesting spin to the trio that moved forward on the idea of prison profiteering. However, Don Hutto's background is exceptionally questionable as qualified to lead the emergence of prison reform. Sure, Hutto has extensive history in corrections, but that certainly doesn't mean it has been bright, legal, ethical, or replicable. Hutto worked in many southern states' correctional facilities, with a long history of controversial hires and unconstitutional methods of punishing inmates. [9] Of course, Hutto was interested in furthering the oppression of young black males, being that before he co-founded CoreCivic, he lived on and ran prison plantations from Texas to Arkansas. His cotton plantation was the size of Manhattan with predominantly black inmates.[10] His racist and oppressive history coupled with a rocky career afforded him the title of president for the

American Correction Association and became a co-founder of CoreCivic. Hutto's background depicts that the need for power had a lot of influence in his part of the trio.

So what does all this mean? Three men set out to build a business off the backs of vulnerable people stemming from their educational and historical backgrounds with the criminal justice system. They used their financial and political power to gain advantage on a system that needed a solution, promising to solve a problem that they, in fact, made worse. Instead of demonstrating empathy toward those directly affected, they showed apathy and chose their financial gains over the lives and generations of people lost to a broken system. CoreCivic often states there aren't enough private prisons to negatively impact the larger issue of mass incarceration. However, after watching people needlessly die beside me, I would readily argue that one privately owned prison is simply one too many. Following the money reveals the scheme that has led to mass incarceration in America. Privatization of prisons enhances the problem as it provides voter buy-outs on the legislative and congressional level, down to district courts. Lawmakers, decision-makers, judges, court-appointed attorneys, sheriffs, prison guards and staff all flow through the chain of command that reap the benefits of more prisoners behind bars. Individual, corporate, and private investors get their financial share also through fronting costs or buying stocks. Meanwhile, taxpayers and inmates pay the highest expense because society isn't safer, and prisoners aren't rehabilitated for re-entry into society. We've talked about the money; now, let's talk about why this all matters.

CHAPTER 4:
WHY DOES THIS MATTER?

"Prison walls have a double function: to lock people in and the public out." - Manfred Nowak

---

Mass incarceration plaguing American society matters for one central reason - you. It matters because *you* matter. This issue is bigger than me and the millions of other incarcerated individuals. While prisoners are outcast from society, the issue of mass incarceration is not. It is prevalent and negatively impacts every member of our society directly or indirectly. When we follow the money that manufactures mass incarceration, we find the wealthiest of our nation in partnership with the lawmakers of our nation deciding where federal dollars go. Unfortunately, those dollars are largely going to fund mass incarceration. Next, there is the hard-working tax-paying middle class that is completely consumed with working full-time jobs and providing for their families that they have no time to fight for or against political issues, despite the fact they are largely responsible for providing the funds that lawmakers use to fund these systems. Last, there is the poor of society that has to fight and struggle to meet basic needs. They are most vulnerable to the systems of mass incarceration, crime, and entanglement with the criminal justice system. That is how I got here. Poor, uneducated, no stability, no role models, mentors, or guidance, and I had no hope for anything greater - only unmet needs. This chapter would digress to discuss the multitude of ways mass incarceration has etched itself into the fabric of society, permitting an acceptable environment for the continued mistreatment of those incarcerated, so I will stay focused.

And still, it is clear who mass incarceration impacts most directly - the masses that are incarcerated. Prisoners receive the most brutal effects of being a part of this system. The previous chapters laid out the direct effects of physical, psychological, and emotional effects beyond punishment for crime. In the same regard, the impacts of mass incarceration go far beyond inmates.

Families of the Masses

No one considers the impact mass incarceration has on the family and the family structure. It is often said that when one member of the family does time, everyone suffers the consequences. Families are the core of our society. Without healthy and strong families, we will see a repeat of generational incarceration. Families are torn apart when one or both parents are ensnared with the justice system. It is a difficult, oppressive web that functions much like a black hole. It is extremely easy to get into, and extremely difficult to get out of.

The financial, social, and emotional impact on families is overwhelming and the costs continue to compound even after their loved one has returned home. The aftermath of mass incarceration, as it reverberates back into society, should be acknowledged as a human rights issue. Advocacy organizations primarily focus on the violation of inmates' human rights, and rightfully so. However, the evidence of the impact on families is devastating, creating a larger problem for society.

The research is astounding. With over five million children experiencing an incarcerated parent at one point in their life, 92% of those incarcerated individuals are fathers, with the rates of mothers steadily increasing. One study found that children with incarcerated fathers are more likely to display behavioral issues such as acting out and depression when their father is imprisoned between their third and ninth birthday. Further, this increases the likelihood that those children will experience juvenile delinquency. Because lower socioeconomic black men are five times more likely to be incarcerated than anyone else, many black boys and girls are left without a father figure.

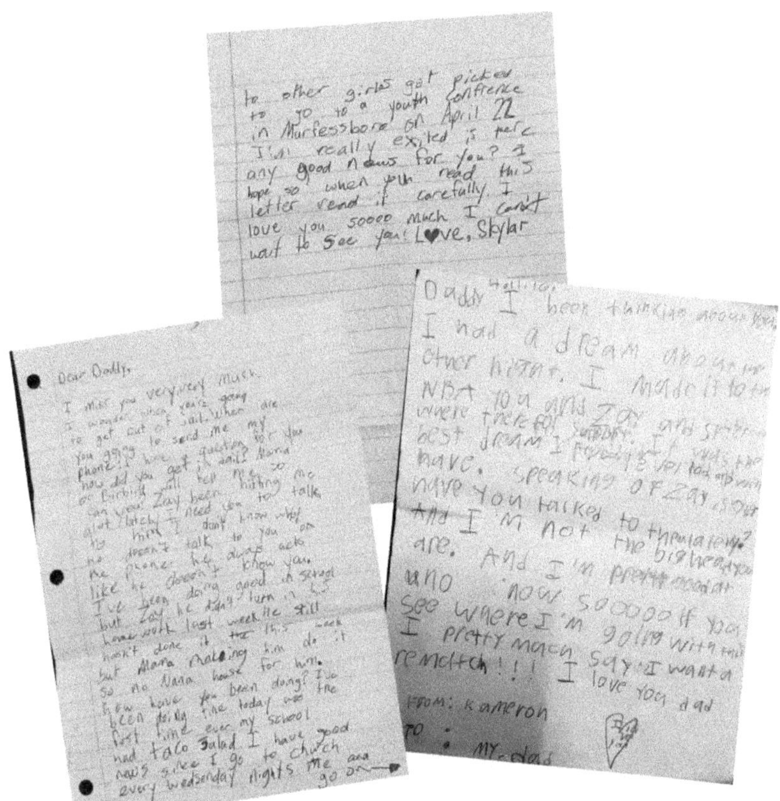

My life

As I sat in trial, I knew that my fate was sealed when I looked over at my mom and saw tears slide down her face. I had no idea what that moment would be in its magnitude, but I quickly discovered that this sentence affected more than me.

Being a father is the proudest role of my life. There is nothing I wouldn't give to have my children living lives that are full of potential, passion, and most importantly, provision. There are many days and many nights that I sit and wonder what our lives would be like if I received a fair trial to begin with. I wonder what our experiences would be if I was truly treated as "innocent until proven guilty," and received the support I needed to fight my case (as opposed to feeling like a system was fighting me). My mind often wanders on what it would have been like to be at their birthday parties, or to pick them up from school when they're having a bad day, or to be there to tuck them in at night. It is infuriating to meditate on how many days have been robbed from me, and from them, because of a systematic failure that I now know erred further away from a mistake, and more towards intention. I try, as best as I am able, to communicate my love and presence in their life, but there is still a void that they experience without me. This is the situation for me and so many other incarcerated individuals.

Reflecting on my family history, I fell privy to the effects of intergenerational incarceration as well. My mom's drug addiction landed her in and out of jail for petty crimes. My father did his fair share of prison time long before I was ever born. In recognizing the effects of my father's absence, I passionately pursue an active presence in my children's life so that the effects aren't as detrimental.

Beyond my family, there was a constant battle between my community and the police growing up. It is no secret that over-policing is an institutional issue. I would consider this the "front lines" of mass incarceration. Distrust was learned early as I watched the cops shake down black and brown people simply for existing. I recall police swooning my neighborhood like flies on a carcass looking for a wrong blink of an individual to assert unconstitutional authority. People were constantly being stalked and harassed for no legally justifiable reason at all. The battle for survival mixed with avoidance of the law created a cesspool of prototypical people that would easily be cast away to "the system." Essentially, all the broken families negatively impacted by intergenerational incarceration, poverty, lack of education and resources create broken communities that are burdened by unbearable troubles and hunted as prey to the system of mass incarceration. We must consider the reality that's created when those who are facing the most troubles become society's trouble.

Society's trouble as troubling

Because families are negatively affected by mass incarceration, our society experiences the rippling economic and social effects. We have followed the dollars that land big bucks in the pockets of lawmakers, but the resounding impact lies within society. Plainly stated:

It matters that families are being torn apart by unjust systems that gain profit by their ability to lock up more people.

It matters that lives are needlessly taken by systems that could re-shape their trajectory.

It matters that crimes of survival are being committed for basic resources.

It matters that crime and punishment have become a profitable industry as opposed to a system of correction.

It matters that institutionalized racism continues to sustain mass incarceration.

It matters that prison profiteering has emerged from a local town to a global giant.

It matters that a lack of a fair trial, coupled with unjust sentences, are depleting entire communities of hope.

It matters that families, communities, and generations are being destroyed by excessive incarceration.

It matters that taxpayers are wasting billions upon billions of dollars every year when those same dollars could go toward effective solutions to the problem.

Not only does *it* matter, but *you* matter. Because you matter, the issue of mass incarceration should matter to you. There is no question as to whether the issue of mass incarceration *should* matter to anyone. Regardless of any race (political or ethnic), role (inside or outside society), status, creed, or religion, there are mounds of information and supporting activists that speak to why this matters. This happens to be one of those resources.

Once the conversation moves from the wealthy versus the poor, the powerful versus the powerless, and the prominent and popular versus the forgotten, to America versus Mass Incarceration, we will see systemic change that will break the racially motivated funnel that has so many people incarcerated. Dissecting the issue of mass incarceration flows beyond the current of the money and seeps its way into the fabric of our hearts. The invisible forces of equity and justice are the fuel that keep this money-hungry engine flowing. Allow me to explain.

PART II:
EQUITY & JUSTICE FOR
ALL

Rivera L. Peoples

CHAPTER 5:
EQUITY VS. EQUALITY

"Equality is giving everyone a shoe. Equity is giving everyone a shoe that fits."
- Dr. Naheed Dosani

Equity is the form of fairness and impartiality. The criminal justice system indirectly implies that it uses equitable practices by often using the term 'equality' to represent how they do what they do. Much of the gap between what is said and the conditions of the way things are lies within equity. *Trust me, I know.* I'm here every day when our constitutional rights as human beings are denied, people are beaten, raped, robbed, and denied medical attention by corrupt prison officials that abuse power and language to cover their tracks. I've seen unimaginable realities of what actually happens. Equitable practices guarantee that everyone has access to the same opportunities. In reality, the system of checks and balances defaults to oppressive forms of equality. And actually, that's generous to say. In some cases, nothing is done at all.

In the cold cruel world of horrendous prison conditions, equity is not a reality. It's actually so far from a reality that corruption reigns as the norm. It's *expected* that inmates won't be treated right, that guards will participate in dishonest and shameful activities, and that a small remnant of hope will be found in the occasional structure of compliance that constitutes order.

Many Americans are led to believe that this is normal and should be accepted. Have you ever heard, "If you do the crime, you do the time?" Interlaced within this statement is the subconscious acceptance that whatever happens within prison walls is justifiable because, after all, the inmate is guilty and should face the consequences. Although this is one example, the American public is perpetually socialized to simultaneously accept and ignore the horrors that happen behind these walls. Propaganda statements like this can be debunked with ease because what if the inmate is *not* guilty? The premise that the time served is acceptably deplorable and inhumane is the foundational reason why there hasn't been change to the criminal justice system. Statements like these are weak deterrents of crime and falsifications of the entirety of what that 'time' looks like. Further, we must recognize that the lack of equitable practices within the criminal justice system stems from racially motivated oppression and financial gain.

You've got that right. Race and money within the evolution of the criminal justice system are fundamental to the inequitable practices that are often ignored. Not to belabor the point of the historical foundations (see previous section), but let's pay attention to how this is displayed in the world today. Let's take a look at the impact of financial and racial equity.

Financial equity

The dollars always must be assessed. We certainly have to look to the money trail to unveil how cash flow has impacted decision-making. Poverty is no hidden issue and it's certainly not going anywhere. Jesus told His disciples in Matthew 26:11 that, "The poor will always be among us," and there is no truer statement about socioeconomic statuses in America.[1] There's no need in arguing the expanse of poverty, or the diminishing of poverty, or even to compare the different types of poverty. Poverty is a prevalent issue that has consistently existed across time, and will continue to exist. By definition, poverty means the state of one who lacks a usual or socially acceptable amount of money or material possessions.[2]

Because poverty isn't going anywhere, those who *aren't* poor have a moral obligation to treat those who are poor with decent human regard. The truth is that countless millions of other inmates and I were not and are not treated decently, fairly, and certainly not with equity. The rate of incarcerating the poor and underprivileged is modern day oppression.

Let me explain. The process of detainment, litigation, and incarceration are not free rides to food and shelter. These processes are substantial financial burdens on families that already experience financial hardship. The navigation from arrest to reentry exploits the most vulnerable because of the cost of goods, services, and products that are required to navigate the path of freedom. Plainly stated, poor people are subjugated to incarceration because they lack the means to financially navigate the system. I know this from experience, and the Consumer Financial Protection Bureau (CFPB) agrees that my experience wasn't an isolated incident. According to the CFPB 2022 Financial Marketplace Report, the criminal justice system is failing at recidivism because (1) for-profit and private companies are embedded throughout the criminal justice process and charging high costs for services that have been historically free; (2) consumers (in this case, inmates and their supporting loved ones) have no control over which service provider they use; and, (3) failure to pay fines and fees result in harsh consequences (further aggrieving their circumstances) causing the individual or loved one to make sacrifices.[3]

According to a report of aggregated data from the Bureau of Justice statistics, the majority of incarcerated people were poor upon pre-incarceration. In 2014, there was a median annual income of $19,650 prior to their arrest.[4] Based on my experience, that's pretty high income. That statistic assumes there was something more than government assistance that had to be divided by seven hungry people. My family and I were already experiencing financial hardship, so I was poor upon my arrest and could not afford a lawyer. I was assigned a court-appointed attorney. Since my time of being in, I have discovered many people's financial situation that looked like mine. In all of my prison stays, I seldomly meet wealthy people. The men here come from inner-city single-parent homes from poverty-stricken neighborhoods with no additional financial support. I recognized this was more than a coincidence, and research supports this observation.

Poor people are disadvantaged by the criminal justice system before they are ever arrested. Researching this taught me that my experiences are consistent with what's happening nationwide. I grew up in the government housing projects with access to public education that had no influence in my life because I had a drug-abusing mom, an absent alcoholic father, and hungry siblings that formed my family structure. My grandmother served as an adult presence, but she was overloaded with the care of three generations. At any given time, that was eight people living in a one-bedroom apartment - and the door was revolving. There was no consistent, stable income. We only had government assistance that assisted but did not, and could not, fully support. The impacts of being ostracized financially only added to the impoverished experience of my upbringing. I loved sports like every other kid in America, but where was the consistent ride to practice? Or even the registration fees to participate? I needed help in the classroom, but where was the money for a tutor? Or the safe, quiet space to focus on my homework? How could I focus on homework when I came home to no food to eat and the lights off? Do you get the picture? There are too many elements to fully explain how poverty affects every area of life, but these are a few examples from my background.

As mentioned, the financial burden doesn't stop with litigation and incarceration. Inmates are economically crippled by job stigmatization and remaining under community control (probation, community service, house arrest, etc.) after time served. These barriers after serving time compound the financial ability of inmates to gain employment. To make matters worse, the same family and support system that struggled to maintain the costs of support during incarceration are faced with the financial and emotional burden of supporting this same loved one post-incarceration. This burden is too heavy for poor people, and most opt to take the consequences for unpaid fines and fees, choose to flee from the law, which deepens their consequences, or turn back to a life of crime in hopes that they are able to afford the financial demands of their freedom.

Poverty has a way of making life a grim reality, and as a young black boy that fit the statistics, I was a prime candidate for the criminal justice system to devour. I firmly believe my race, an African American male, played a major role in my trial and sentencing.

Racial Equity

Race in the criminal justice system plays an intricate part in feeding the beast of the criminal justice system. Why is that? Because if the imprisonment numbers of black and minority people were not as outrageous, there would be no need for the continual building of more prisons, no need for additional funding for these buildings, and essentially, no overwhelm of federal and state prison systems creating the need for private prison systems. Prison profiteering and capitalization on required goods and services remain a culprit in adding to the financial and racial inequity that populates prisons. It is no secret that racial equity is non-existent to the American criminal justice system. Key findings from The Sentencing Project's data make these facts evident:

- Black Americans are incarcerated in state prisons at nearly 5 times the rate of white Americans.
- Nationally, one in 81 Black adults in the U.S. is serving time in state prison. Wisconsin leads the nation in Black imprisonment rates; one of every 36 Black Wisconsinites is in prison.
- In 12 states, more than half the prison population is Black: Alabama, Delaware, Georgia, Illinois, Louisiana, Maryland, Michigan, Mississippi, New Jersey, North Carolina, South Carolina, and Virginia.
- Seven states maintain a Black/white disparity larger than 9 to 1: California, Connecticut, Iowa, Maine, Minnesota, New Jersey, and Wisconsin.
- Latinx individuals are incarcerated in state prisons at a rate that is 1.3 times the incarceration rate of whites. Ethnic disparities are highest in Massachusetts, which reports an ethnic differential of 4.1:1.

Racial disparity within incarceration is an evident issue that needs resolving fast. Countless black men, women, and other minorities experience harsher consequences and lengthier sentences simply because of their race and/or ethnicity. Racial disparity in incarceration stems from outdated policy that created a hypervigilance and paranoia towards black men, along with practices and decision-making within prison facilities that perpetuates this thinking.

I know that I'm not the first, but let me certainly not be the last to say, "It's not okay." Racial disparities have plagued our country for centuries, and they are continuing to cripple the black community and family structure. No one is by any means excusing criminal behavior because of race. However, we have to move from assuming guilt because of race, and even more, we must move from creating havoc in impoverished neighborhoods by "stop and frisk" tactics or racially profiled assumptions because of over-policing.

I can vividly recall always having a predatory relationship with the police. I call it a predatory relationship because it felt like sharks in a goldfish bowl waiting to swarm and pounce on their prey - us. They were constantly circling the block, stopping people because they simply felt like it, and looking for crime, trouble, and disrespect to provoke action. There was no class or formal instruction, but you just simply knew as a custom to avoid the police, to be quiet in their presence, and to get out of their presence as quickly as possible. This reality wasn't mine alone. Everyone in my neighborhood held this same belief system. We all knew that simply being black made us prey, but it wasn't until I learned about economics that I learned being poor made us the most edible.

That may be hard to fathom, but the statistics show it plainly. According to the Prison Policy Initiative, being black and poor is the target profile for incarceration. At the time of arrest, black men are the poorest among all races with a median income of $17,625 while maintaining the highest incarceration rate. The racial disparities take place long before arrest and are heavily perpetuated throughout every stage in the process of the system. This book doesn't have the capacity to discuss the gross disregard for black and minority life, so pick any area of the system to be explored and I guarantee the facts will support that statement. The unfortunate truth is that my experience is not an isolated incident. Moreso, there are lawmakers and decision-makers that recognize I am one of many who fit the profile of their profit.

Educational Equity

The state of poverty isn't *only* limited to race and money. It's ugly that this gets worse, but ignorance is an underlying issue that keeps this engine running. Lack of education is a glaring endemic among those most often massively incarcerated. I beat the statistical odds as it relates to having received a high school diploma, but most of those who are incarcerated at large do not finish high school. Research shows roughly 70% of state prisoners do not have a high school diploma with the average level of education attained being at 10th grade. This should come as no surprise as history has lent itself toward the trend of abusing the lowest of our society. Take a look at the following chart that shows the percentage of men aged 20-34 in prison or jail categorized by race and education compared from 1980 to 2008.

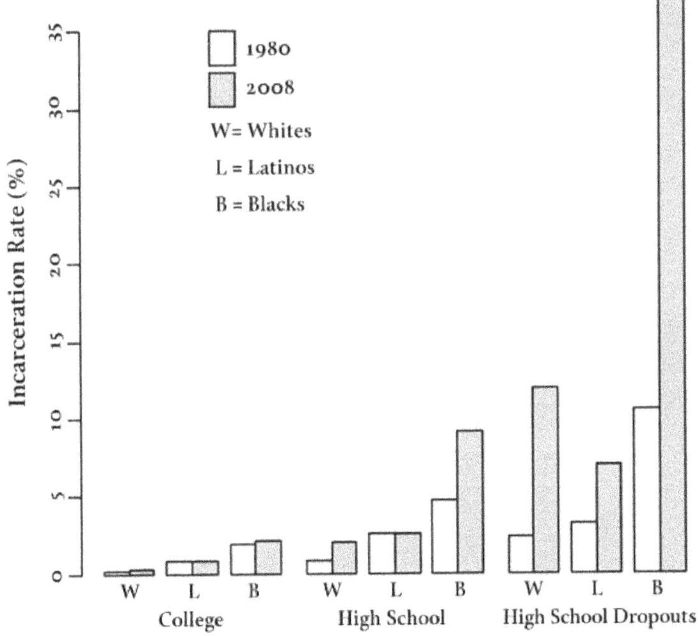

Source: Becky Pettit, Bryan Sykes, and Bruce Western, "Technical Report on Revised Population Estimates and NLSY79 Analysis Tables for the Pew Public Safety and Mobility Project" (Harvard University, 2009).[10]

Need I remind you that I graduated high school in 2009? Though we are many years removed from this timeframe, the systemic structures still stand to repeat this process.

Education, or a lack thereof, makes for a prime candidate of mass incarceration. Our society rewards more knowledge with increased potential for higher social status. Plainly stated, there's a higher income-earning potential, more access to resources, tax benefits and deductions, and an overall better quality of life with more education. While the rewards for more education are a prize in this country, no one is discussing the punishment for less education.

I went to an inner-city public school. Not only was the funding for this school low, but the morale was as well. There have been many studies done on the school-to-prison pipeline, and I can say that those experiences share a part of my reality. I saw young black boys get in more trouble than any of the other kids growing up. I witnessed friends come back to the classroom and not have a clue what we were learning, so they stopped trying. I witnessed kids get suspended so much that it led to drop-outs, teenage parenthood, and exposure to other violence and life trauma. I wasn't a saint in the classroom, but I was certainly observant. I watched the interest in school fade to the back of many kids' minds as they sought to figure out how to live. I was one of them. What made me different from those around me was that I saw the finish line worth striving for. None of my siblings or family members, for that matter, finished high school, and in that regard, I wanted to change the narrative. Although I was able to graduate, can we truly say I overcame it? Yes, I achieved the first level of readily available and state-mandated education requirements, but what did that actually mean to the long run of my life? I was still impoverished with no access to information to change the situation that I was surrounded by. I was still left alone in a world with no guidance, no knowledge, no skill set, and unfortunately, no hope.

This is not a sob story for my predicament, but I only imagine what my life would be like had I simply known more. I am not the only one plagued by a lack of education and information. I differentiate here because, most times, education alone does not fix life problems. For example, it did me no good to learn the process of photosynthesis from biology class while I was simultaneously trying to figure out how my siblings and I would bathe because there was no water at home. Correctional populations at large reflect this (as previously depicted). Furthermore, information is what unveiled my unfair trial and other resources that should be available to me as an inmate. Information is what has transformed my thinking and my belief system about life as is. I'm grateful for the education and the information that I have been afforded during my incarceration, but if I could re-write my narrative, it would include both information and education with support to first meet basic life needs.

The problem remains that the numbers are evident. The data has been consistent since the inception of prison as a means of correction; yet, little progress has been made.

There have been steps in the right direction, but the constant battle of progression and regression continues to stop true forward momentum. Nothing about my experience has been equitable as it should be, per my constitutional and human rights. And unfortunately, nothing about my reality reflects what it should be, had I at least received a fair trial to start.

The fundamental problem with the criminal justice system is that it relies on *people* within the system to employ and enforce equitable practices. Inherently, people are not (always) the problem, but the lack of accountability, coupled with corrupt motives, hidden agendas, and money behind the matter, permits those very people to carry out an alternative agenda. Hence, that is why two justice systems simultaneously take place. One serves and protects, while another enslaves and neglects. From a larger perspective, those same people *are* the law. They are the very embodiment of the governmental constructs that provide order, guidelines, and safety to our society. Who is higher than the law? Who does one turn to in America when the law acts lawless? Or yet, when the law doesn't apply to the enforcers of the law? What is to happen when the lawmakers become the lawbreakers? We have to stop turning a blind eye to the power that this invisible system has in using racial, economic, and educational disparities to feed the beast of mass incarceration.

Change begins when we expose those characters who have a part in feeding the beast while holding representation accountable to equitable practices that uphold the essence of life and liberty for *all,* and not treating inmates like the exception to the clause of the 13th amendment. It's interesting that, historically, criminals were called outlaws, yet criminals are still fighting for protections *out*side of the very law that is to protect them. This gap between the law and the assumed lawless rests in proper representation. Representation failed me, and the whole of this book explains why.

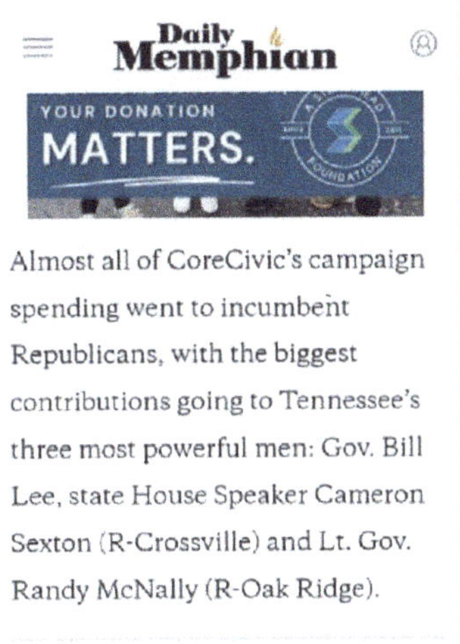

Almost all of CoreCivic's campaign spending went to incumbent Republicans, with the biggest contributions going to Tennessee's three most powerful men: Gov. Bill Lee, state House Speaker Cameron Sexton (R-Crossville) and Lt. Gov. Randy McNally (R-Oak Ridge).

Preventing crime before anyone ends up in prison would prevent profit and is bad for business. CoreCivic has contributed more to Tennessee's politicians than most other entities and has spent a significant amount on lobbying for mass incarceration. When you follow the money, the scheme is always revealed.

Sexton says he's not opposed to criminal justice reform — including to prevent crimes before anyone ends up in prison. But he says that's a conversation for another year.

Tennessee House Speaker Cameron Sexton says, "I'm not opposed to criminal justice reform — including to prevent crimes before anyone ends up in prison, but that's a conversation for another year."

CHAPTER 6:
THE 14TH AMEND(ED)

"No one truly knows a nation until one has been inside its jails. A nation should not be judged by how it treats its highest citizens but its lowest ones."

- Nelson Mandela

I was wrongfully convicted of First-degree murder and received a sentence of life with the possibility of parole after 51 years, plus 100 years for robbery and kidnapping. I was prosecuted and convicted of being criminally responsible for the conduct of another person. Do you know what that means? It means that I am sentenced to serve all of this time because of the actions of someone else.

One of the largest issues with the criminal justice system is that society is made to believe that injustice only happens at the final verdict that seals the fate of the accused. I quickly learned this was a terrible lie that is used to rationalize the outcome of complex cases and give harsher sentences. The system is too large with too many processes in place to lay the weight of the verdict on closing moments. Although every moment is critical, the crucial moments don't begin with the trial, judge, and sentencing - crucial moments end there. Deciding factors are culminating long before that, and this is why it "just ain't justice" for a lot of young, poor black boys.

Unfortunately, my story is one of many. I became a victim of the *in*justice system because I did not receive a fair trial. I was originally charged with first-degree murder, attempted second-degree murder, and employment of a firearm during a dangerous felony. After one round of litigation, I received a superseding charge that indicted me with a primary offense of first-degree murder and added other defendants. This complicated matters.

All of these processes were new to me. I had never been accused of a crime, and even more, facing charges that I didn't understand. I was a child that needed more than my mommy. I needed help to make sense of all that was being thrown my way. Because of my impoverished condition, I was assigned a court-appointed lawyer at my arraignment. I was frustrated about the situation I was in, but I was excited to collaborate with my lawyer so that I could give him all the information he needed to help me get out of this bad jam. Except...he never showed.

I sat waiting for days on end. I wondered when he would come. I would ask if there was any mail for me. I contacted my family to see if they heard anything. I periodically asked the guards if I missed any correspondence or communication. As the days got longer with no contact whatsoever from him, I began to worry deeply. I found myself pacing anxiously while trying to remain hopeful that there was some mix-up, and he would visit me so that we could meet before trial. I gave myself every excuse in the world. Maybe the day went long, and he forgot. Maybe he was misinformed on where I was and was trying to schedule a visitation. Maybe he was busy researching and getting all of the facts together so that when we did meet, it wasn't a waste of time. Maybe he had a personal emergency, and it's delaying him contacting me. No matter which excuse gave me temporary relief, I was still unsettled each day that went by without me preparing for what would be a pivotal day in my life. The days got longer and simultaneously closer to my trial date. Sadly enough, even in that predicament, I didn't know how to advocate for myself. The time was winding down and I still hadn't met with him. Who was this guy, anyway? What did he look like? What was his courtroom experience? Is he so good that he can be a last-minute savior? Or, is he so bad that he avoids doing his job? I had so many questions with no one to tell, "Hey, my trial is coming up and I still haven't met with my lawyer."

The days came and went by until the night before trial. I have never felt such an awful mix of emotions. My mind raced a million miles an hour at what could or could not take place in the courtroom. I just knew that I had to remain positive and hopeful. It was hard to expect a win from a battle I didn't know how to fight, or even more, *who* was on my team that would be fighting with me.

In the state of Tennessee, my alleged charge of First-degree murder is a capital offense. No matter what it was deemed, I knew that there were only two outcomes of this trial - I served time, or I didn't. My pre-trial time was agonizing enough, and I couldn't imagine having to spend more time away from my family and my children. The questions ran at the speed of light through my mind as I tried to keep my composure. The time had come, and I was escorted to the courtroom.

The trial commenced and I was in the courtroom, placed behind this table next to a man I had never spoken to a day in my life. His name was Nathan Moore - my court-appointed defense counsel. This total stranger was the voice that was responsible for advocating my freedom. All of those emotions began to boil on the inside of me. How could he defend me when he never heard my story? How could he stand in my stead and tell the judge and jury my truth when he didn't know it, because he never met with me for it? How is this even allowed? The pressure from these boiling thoughts made me uncomfortable in my seat. There were legal protocols and jargon being thrown all around me, and it was vital for my future. I saw my mother in the courtroom, and the physical distance by which we were separated reminded me of the continued distance I could face as a result of this trial. The magnitude of those opening moments welled up in me to where I could no longer sit silent. After all, what else did I have to lose?

I spoke up to the judge and informed her that I had not met with Mr. Moore, and that I didn't agree with the way he was representing me. I informed the court that Mr. Moore was not listening to my concerns or what I was trying to present as my defense. He had no regard for what I was trying to say. Who knew that the deafening power of silence would continue to suffocate my chance at freedom. In so many words, the judge informed me that I had two options. I could "sit there, shut up, and behave" or I would be put in the back of the courtroom; either way, the trial would continue. So, against my wishes, I conceded. I sat there and I listened to my defense counsel do nothing in my favor. Long before my conviction was ever rendered, I was guilty of believing in a system that was never designed to deliver me justice.

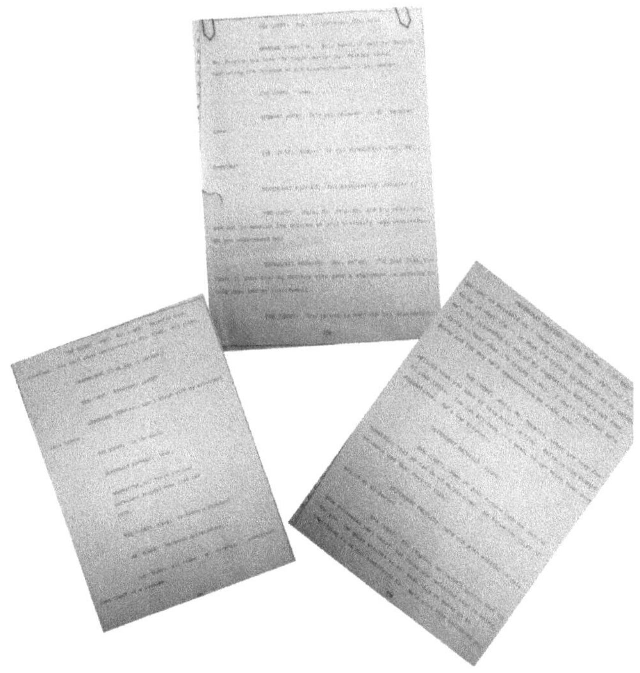

At the time, I had no knowledge that it was my 13th amendment constitutional rights that were being violated in the real time of my trial proceedings. All I knew is that it simply wasn't right for Mr. Moore to defend me when we had never met. Although I took the very bold step to speak up concerning this miscarriage of justice, the court and its residing power stopped my pursuit with no remorse.

That was my first step to defend myself, but it certainly wasn't my last. Post-conviction, I immediately began the fight of my life. I learned of my constitutional rights and began the process of self-advocacy. I continued to speak up, and so did my court-appointed attorney. Under oath, with a potential penalty of perjury, Nathan Moore admitted that he directly disobeyed the law by not meeting with me or visiting me prior to my trial and conviction. Additionally, he admitted that the minimal amount of attention given to this capital case was done in the loudest, busiest part of the courtroom, in-between his other cases. Since, I have several grounds for relief stemming from his lack of counsel:

- Nathan Moore did not, in any way, consult me for my defense.
- I did not state or agree to anything that could incriminate me any further.
- Key witness Brian Moreland recanted his trial testimony post-conviction (his testimony was key in my conviction).

The most troubling part of this ordeal is that they knew the law. Every character in my story had an obligation to obey the constitution as set forth, but they failed me. The lawyer knew he had an obligation to meet with me or request another trial date. The court knew that they had an obligation to explore my concern. At the very minimum, empathy could have been displayed to allow for a full expression or investigation of my willingness to speak up about my defense, but the harsh reality that I learned for the first time is that there is the 14th amendment, and the 14 amended. The 14th amendment is explained above, but the

14 amend*ed* is what I experienced that day and every day of this process for the last thirteen years and counting. The amended version of the 14th amendment is the treatment of the poor, unprivileged citizens of American society. This amended version is the version that does not apply to the wealthy, the powerful, the socially, racially, academically, and otherwise privileged. It applies to those who statistically, racially, and economically look like me.

The system works to suffocate the one thing poor people don't have. Poor people don't have a voice. They have no power or influence to grant them rights or access so that their voice of reason, concern, or interest can be heard. They don't have the resources or affluence to persuade lawmakers or decision-makers that favor their impoverished condition. They don't have the means to speak up or to change their circumstances. All they have in this country is their voice, and when that's all that there is, it is easy to suppress. Because poor people lack the means to defend themselves, they must be represented by those who can speak for them.

Representing the Amended 14th

Proper legal aid and assistance is the main component of the 6th amendment. It also ensures that those unable to afford counsel have a chance at a fair trial by being *properly* represented. However, it is simply not enough to merely be assigned an attorney. The problem remains that representation from court-appointed counsel becomes a matter of making money, as opposed to administering the law so that equitable practices can be upheld while fair decisions and verdicts are made. In hindsight, I learned that court-appointed counsel fulfilled the extent of the law that I was given representation, but I had to learn, in the cruelest circumstances possible, exactly *what* was being represented. Mr. Moore was assigned to my case to be my defense, but I had to learn he wasn't assigned to protect me. He was protecting himself and an invisible system that was at work to benefit all of the participating characters. After spending time inside, I came to learn that there are many characters that participate in benefitting from this invisible system at the expense of the poor. I wasn't the only one who became an object to this game.

Despite my lack of representation and many nights after my sentencing, everyone who processed my case from arraignment through my journey of several prison institutions has gotten paid - and paid well. The judge, the jury, the bailiffs, the prosecutors, the clerical staff, the prison guards, and all the personnel in-between, along with the investors of the private institutions. According to the United States Federal Government register, the cost of incarceration for a federal inmate was $39,158 for the year 2020. This figure breaks down to $120.59 per day. There are millions of prisoners that are serving long sentences, and this is why prison profiteering is a billion-dollar industry. To date, I've been incarcerated for 13 years, and the math is astonishing. My time in prison has generated over half a million dollars. Doesn't that sound like job security? Like someone would be well paid for a very long time because federal and private dollars need bodies in cells? It's hard to process that my life could be worth so much in such an awful way. Lengthy prison stays aren't the only money-makers, as I was held un-convicted for almost 15 months, just like many others. In this country, young, black men are 50% more likely to be held in custody *before* trial than are white defendants. Regardless of race, the amount of un-convicted individuals detained pretrial is steadily increasing. Why? Because it *pays* for people to be in jail. Day and night, I wonder how it's remotely justifiable for me to spend this much time inside without having received a fair trial. I find more and more that the ugly truth is that I am not alone.

Roughly half a million people are currently jailed as they await trial. Many critics argue that this is because the accused cannot afford bail. However, bail bonding is not a scotch-free fix to this issue either, being that for-profit companies have intervened into the criminal justice system processes with the same interest in mind - money. There are for-profit companies that issue bail bonds if the accused is unable to pay for their release. Of course, my impoverished condition fell into the category of having to wait for trial under prison watch. It should be no shock that more people in jail means there is more federal and private funding for local and county facilities that temporarily house these individuals.

Just Ain't Justice

The handling of my case and the outcome were not a coincidence. There are too many people that look like me, in more than one way, for anyone with any sort of reasoning ability to believe that happenstance has claimed my fate. It is the entirety of the invisible system at work that needs individuals like me to have the title, "criminal." Many of those inside with me will testify that they, too, received little to no help from their court-appointed lawyers, and were denied valuable information that could have transformed the outcome of their trial. I will stand before God and any man to inform them that my sentencing is unjust, outrageous, and unfit. I am not some wicked and atrocious monster that deserves to be caged wrongfully. The word "criminal" is not a word used much here on the inside, but it permeates every aspect of our identity, while constantly reminding us that the identity of a criminal justifies every harsh, unusual, and awful deed done to us as permissible. And I'm expected to believe that a person who is unfairly mistreated by the very ones designed to protect them will receive justice? This is why criminal "justice" feels more like, "criminally legal," "criminal castaways," or "criminal verdicts."

How is it that someone can be up against a first-degree murder charge with a lawyer who refuses to meet with them to prepare for the case. And I'm expected to believe in the justice system? My experiences make me wonder, *'What is criminal justice?'*. Why is this system called criminal *justice?* I can think of a lot of names that are more fitting to my experiences, the facts, and the masses of people who are daily (directly and indirectly) impacted by this system. Cornell Law School states criminal justice is "a generic term that refers to the laws, procedures, institutions, and policies at play before, during, and after the commission of a crime." According to the University of Massachusetts Global, the criminal justice system is comprised of three parts, (law enforcement, court system, and corrections), while being defined as, "the structure of laws, rules, and agencies designed to hold criminals accountable for their misdeeds and help them to restore their victims as much as possible". The list of definitions goes on but in my humble and well experienced opinion, there is no justice for the one deemed a criminal. According to the Constitution of the United States, the criminal justice systems' purpose is designed to deliver "justice" for all; except, "all" here is not inclusive. Our country has a history of being selective of who it serves and protects and is clear about those who are outside of that scope. Incarceration taught me that those entangled in the criminal justice system aren't considered worthy. The constitutional amendments are primarily responsible for creating the escape clause, by intentional wording, that have created this tremendously profitable mess of millions of lives.

The list of unjust facts don't stop there:

- A Black person is five times more likely to be stopped without just cause than a white person.
- A Black man is twice as likely to be stopped without just cause than a Black woman.
- 65% of Black adults have felt targeted because of their race. Similarly, approximately 35% of Latino and Asian adults have felt targeted because of race.
- 87% of Black adults say the U.S. criminal justice system is more unjust towards Black people; 61% of white adults agree.

I am not an expert at law. I don't have the jurisdictional authority to preside on behalf of the court and, at this current time, I don't have a political appointment that could influence the continuation of laws that make systems like these possible. But what I do know is that there is no justice for criminals when profit motives are at the core of decision-making. There are millions of poor and undereducated people that are being bullied out of their freedom and herded to the slaughter because the system works collectively to strip them of the two things they do have: voice and identity. The poor voice goes unheard, while the identity is shifted to an image of a criminal. American society needs to take a long hard look at all of the amendments in relation to the process of law. They have been amended and represented to create the belly of the biggest beast named criminal justice. Many of the people that I have come in contact with over my prison stays have journeys that look a lot like mine. They've done 20–30-year sentences while fighting for their constitutional rights, freedom, and innocence. Their time is filled with constant paperwork and filing, night terrors, and down days as they await word for their appeals. Many of those same people share my sentiment about justice and its lack of presence in the midst of our situation. There are no greater words for my heart's cry concerning this seemingly insurmountable issue than this open letter I wrote called, *"Justice, Where Are You?"*. This open letter I wrote communicates my passion, mixed with my anger and frustration, while making my claim clear:

"JUSTICE, WHERE WERE YOU??? NO, FUCK THAT. JUSTICE, WHERE ARE YOU!!!!? I KEEP HEARING SO MUCH ABOUT YOU, JUSTICE, AND I'M ALWAYS HOPEFUL THAT YOU WILL SHOW UP!! BUT JUSTICE, WHERE ARE YOU IN THIS JUSTICE SYSTEM??? HOW IS IT EVEN JUSTICELY POSSIBLE TO FACE A JUSTICE SYSTEM WHEN YOU'RE PISS POOR, UNDEREDUCATED, WITH NONE OF THE RESOURCES YOUR OPPONENT POSSESSES. JUST HOW THE JUSTICE SYSTEM WORKS. THE JUSTICE SYSTEM IS WELL-REPRESENTED BY IVY LEAGUE, COLLEGE EDUCATED GRADUATES WITH UNLIMITED SOURCES AND RESOURCES, BUT IT'S THE "JUSTICE SYSTEM," RIGHT? JUSTICE, WHERE ARE YOU? THIS CAN'T BE JUSTICE!! JUSTICE IS DEFINED AS FAIR AND MORAL, BUT WHY IS IT NEVER FAIR WHEN YOU'RE CAUGHT UP IN THE JUSTICE SYSTEM? IT'S NEVER BEEN FAIR FOR ME AND PEOPLE THAT LOOK LIKE ME. THAT'S WHY WE'VE OVER-CROWDED EVERY JAIL, EVERY STATE PRISON, FEDERAL PRISON, AND ESPECIALLY EVERY PRIVATELY OWNED PRISON WHO'S SOLE PURPOSE IS TO PRIORITIZE PROFIT OVER REHABILITATION (BIG BUSINESS). THEY NEED US TO KEEP THEIR BUNKS FILLED SO THEY CAN SEND THEIR CHILDREN TO THOSE IVY LEAGUE SCHOOLS THEY LOVE SO MUCH. IF YOUR FAMILY IS POOR LIKE MINE, IN COURT, THE REPRESENTATION AND

ADVOCACY WE ARE APPOINTED AND SUBJECTED TO IN THE NAME OF "JUSTICE" COULDN'T COMPARE TO THE JUSTICE SYSTEM WELL-REPRESENTED BY SOME WELL-TRAINED AND EXPERIENCED, WELL-EDUCATED LAW SCHOOL GRADUATE IN COMPARISON TO MY 18 YR. OLD, 5 FEET 9 INCHES, 145 POUND FRAME, AND MY HIGH SCHOOL DIPLOMA. BUT WAIT, JUSTICE, WHERE ARE YOU?? JUSTICE, HOW IS IT THAT ME, AND PEOPLE THAT LOOK LIKE ME, REPRESENT THE MINORITY IN THIS COUNTRY (THE LAND OF THE FREE!) THAT PROMISED US THE AMERICAN DREAM, BUT SOMEHOW, WE'RE THE MAJORITY INSIDE THIS JUSTICE SYSTEM (NUMBERS DON'T LIE!)? COMPLETE OPPOSITE WHEN YOU'RE RICH; YOU GET HOWEVER MUCH YOUR RICHES CAN PURCHASE. DON'T BELIEVE ME? JUST FOLLOW THE PRESIDENT ON TWITTER. BUT HOLD UP, JUSTICE, WHERE ARE YOU FOR ME AND PEOPLE THAT LOOK LIKE ME, OR THE PEOPLE THAT'S IN MY TAX BRACKET? IT WAS SAID TO BE JUSTICE FOR ALL, NOT JUSTICE FOR SOME. JUST LIKE MY ANCESTORS AND THOSE THAT LOOKED LIKE US WAS PROMISED 40 ACRES AND A MULE, JUSTICE, WHERE ARE YOU?!"
#freeMYbody... free ouR PEOPLES

CHAPTER 7:
CORRECTIONS AIN'T CORRECTIN'

"They [prisons] are not designed to rehabilitate the inmate, though the public propaganda is that this is their function."
- Malcom X

Recidivism is a big fancy word that means prisoners return to crime or prison after their release. You might think, '*Why would anyone want to go back there?*' The truth is that no one *wants* to be a criminal. No little child dreams of becoming a repeat offender and wearing lifelong labels of "convict," "felon," "inmate," and a host of other awful names. No one *wants* to be labeled the bad guy. No child decides they want to be called by a number across their chest, as opposed to their name. However, I've found in my prison time that many of those who are here committed crimes of survival. They were trying to provide food and shelter for their families, and live with the means they had. No adult who truly committed crime out of survival wanted the outcome of harming themselves, others, or society. Does that justify their actions? Absolutely not, but the impact of being undereducated, impoverished, and back on the street with no support leads one to do what they know - survive by any means necessary. Isn't it amazing how this recurring theme of poverty is a means of survival on one side, and a means of exploitation from the other side of this paradigm? It's a terrible cycle where its power can be broken with a decrease in return to prison.

The National Institute of Justice states that recidivism is a fundamental part of criminal justice. Correctional facilities are tasked with the duty and responsibility to aid the redirection of criminal behavior such that criminals are re-socialized and ready to comply with societal norms and expectations upon release. After all, what good does a correctional facility serve if there is no correction? Numerous sources agree that prisons were originally created as a means of punishment for crime. Since its inception, corrections has been a subsystem of criminal justice intended for this purpose. Lawmakers and decision makers soon realized this wasn't effective, efficient, and was extremely costly as prisoners were unsuccessfully integrating back into society by returning to prison. Several shifts were made to reform correctional facilities to a rehabilitative approach, so that prisoners were receiving a holistic path to a change in behavior. At that time in history, indictments included alternatives to prison, such admission to mental health facilities or drug rehabilitation programs. The same laws and social movements that were for the rehabilitation of prisoners and prison systems reverted back to a crime-punishment approach as the advent of prison populations almost tripled, along with - you guessed it - the privatization of prisons and prison profiteering. Benecchi (2021) said it best, "Defunding rehabilitation in our justice systems directly correlates with the increase in the incarceration rate."

It should be evident by now that high rates of recidivism are profitable. After all, who doesn't love a repeat customer? They're easier to process and much easier to retain. Recidivism rates are a key indicator of the invisible system at work to keep prisoners in bondage to the systems and processes that breed the "ideal clientele." It's obvious that correctional facilities are unsuccessful in their way of functioning to benefit the prison and society. Instead, the broken system *is* functioning properly to refunnel profitable gains (people) back into its systems. Simply put, a decrease in recidivism also means a decrease in profits. It is essential that we move from the power of profit to the power of people to mitigate the issue of criminality.

Therefore recidivism should be viewed holistically. The rehabilitative focus can't solely be on the alleged crime that landed the person back behind bars. There must also be focus on the barriers and lack of resources that contribute to unsuccessful attempts at life beyond prison. However, the system falls short in that it does not always provide equipment and tools for life after prison. It is insane to expect anyone to come out of an unhealthy environment better than how they entered it, especially if they haven't been introduced to anything other than isolation, deprivation, and injustice.

My personal story with recidivism and reentry is different from the informative aim of this chapter. I had no prior arrests, no juvenile record, and no criminally legal involvement at all prior to my current situation. The confounds of my current sentencing technically don't allow for me to see the other side of my conviction because I have a life sentence. Essentially, I am illegally placed here, and they never want me to leave. But that is not the case for the majority of people who enter prisons. In 2020, the most common types of crime were the various types of property crime. That means the majority of people who enter prisons will also exit them.

Because the majority of people are re-entering society, a decrease in recidivism rates matters tremendously. Correctional facilities have accomplished nothing if they only ensure victims that offenders are being held accountable for their crime to only release those offenders in a worse condition back to the same environments and communities.

Faults of Correction

The faults of American correctional facilities are too lengthy for this section, much more a single book. Besides, I've laid bare all of the systematic, social, justice, and legalistic issues that contribute to the pitfalls. It is clear that the different facets of American prison systems are terribly failing on all fronts. The toleration of abuse, corruption, manipulation, and power jockeying combined with overcrowding, understaffing, and inhumane conditions are far beyond control. In a perfect world, we could light a match to every building and walk away to never look back. But because we don't live in a perfect world, we need to take a deeper look at what the issues are, because recidivism rates inform us that we're getting it all wrong.

Recidivism rates in the United States are far from impressive. Measuring recidivism is difficult because program requirements are different across state laws, correctional programs, and jurisdictions. Additionally, reentry can be determined by arrest data, but it is hard to determine if a crime occurred for recidivism. Various sources report different rates of return. The Bureau of Justice Statistics performed a 10-year longitudinal study from 2008-2018, with the data released in 2021. Researchers found that 49% of all offenders had a parole violation, probation violation, or re-arrest within three years of their release. Almost half of those that made it out of the prison systems reentered. Why is that?

POWER VS. POVERTY

There are several factors that contribute to recidivism and re-entry. Would you like to know the strongest predictor of recidivism? You guessed it - poverty. According to a study done by the Department of Justice's Office of Justice Programs, poverty was the number one indicator, among other factors, which led to recidivism and was primarily responsible for re-entry. Other studies report similar findings. For instance, the unemployment rate among incarcerated people is as high as 27%, compared to the national unemployment rate of 3.6%. That makes it almost nine times harder for those previously incarcerated to find work. How does a former criminal with a poor family who is unable to find work do with the need to eat, live, and provide for children? According to the American Civil Liberties Union (ACLU), 75% of formerly incarcerated people are unemployed up to a year after their release. There is a wealth of information that points to lack of money, resources, skills, education, mental and psychiatric needs, job discrimination, and a host of other barriers that hinder, and in most cases cripple, success after prison.

Immediate Solutions

The criminal Justice system has a long way to go towards progress and reform from the beginning of the system to the end. There is a grossly large need for change in the criminal justice system, and the return to prison is a major aspect of that need. Recidivism and Reentry rates are a key indicator that the justice system isn't achieving its main objective of "correcting" behavior.

I would dare say that it's the invisible system's agenda to keep people coming back to prison. Those same impoverished, undereducated, and mentally unhealthy people are released back into the world after being caged with no new skills, knowledge, or abilities to succeed; yet, they are somehow expected to thrive. Despite these obstacles, immediate change can be implemented so that more and more formerly incarcerated individuals experience success as a citizen and are able to reintegrate back into society.

I firmly believe that, one day, I will be able to speak to the needs and desires of recidivism because I will be on the other side of this season of my life. Until I am served justice, I will push for change with my pen. There are actionable steps that can be taken right now to ensure that recidivism and reentry rates are lowered, formerly incarcerated rates are lowered, and those released back into society can experience a healthy and thriving life that doesn't lead to revisiting the system's control.

Five years ago, the Department of Justice introduced several initiatives that contribute to the reform of prisons to reduce recidivism and reentry. Following are the initiatives that I believe deserve the most attention due to the present state of the system's dire condition:

- From day one, identifying an inmate's individualized criminogenic needs.
- Encouraging inmates to develop marketable job skills.
- Prioritizing mental health treatment for inmates.
- Phasing out BOP's use of private prisons.
- Equipping inmates with information and resources as they return to the community.

This book would fail to complete its purpose if it only highlighted the struggles and barriers of those who are inside the walls. The problems that this system creates goes far beyond the walls by keeping those outside of the walls, inside of the system. Change is the only hope that we have to turn the direction of more people falling prey to the traps of the justice system as it is. The next chapter highlights specific calls to action to be a part of the change that prisoners, American society, and the global movement for effective imprisonment needs.

PART III:
THE FUTURE OF POWER

Rivera L. Peoples

CHAPTER 8:
A CALL TO ACTION

"Any time you beg another man to set you free, you will never be free. Freedom is something that you have to do for yourselves."
- *Malcolm x*

I *wish,* time and time again, that I had someone in my life who loved me enough to tell me the truth while also steering me on a path that would help me to achieve my ultimate purpose in life. I am in an unfair, inhumane predicament, and I would not imagine this on my worst enemy. Though I will still achieve my God-ordained purpose, I am taking a hard, long route that I want you (and anyone you love) to avoid. I often have to answer the question concerning what can be done about the system. After exposing so many multidimensional and complex aspects, change may feel impossible, but it's not. If we each do our parts, we will dismantle the powers that be and change our nation's incarceration system.

Change the Law

The first and most obvious step that must be taken is to change the law. There is no way our nation can persist with laws that allow for loopholes that create billion-dollar giants while further oppressing the most vulnerable of its population. Most would consider me crazy to think that I, of all people, could call for a law change. However, I have seen firsthand and experienced the detriments of what our current laws permit. There is no way we can expect any differing outcomes with the same legal precedents in place. The law is the foundation that gives mass incarceration, injustice, and inequitable practices its legal place to profit in America. If the law is changed, then all the systems and processes that enact the law will have to change as well.

You might think it's the sole responsibility of congress, senate, and the judiciary branch to be concerned with law change. You might also subconsciously believe that because you don't have a seat of power that you cannot change the law, but that is simply not true. Our democracy gives us so many opportunities to impact the change of law. Here are a few ideas that come to mind:

- Advocacy in the form of signing petitions or joining forces with a social movement.
- Supporting the legislation in your voting jurisdiction that supports the initiatives of change we wish to see.
- Financial involvement through giving to nonprofits focused on at-risk youth or donating to organizations that provide

educational supplies and resources to those incarcerated

- Voting for legislators that have a proven track record of positively impacting incarceration and, likewise, steering away from politicians who are in favor of the continuation of private prisons (remember Hutto, Beasley, and Crants).

There are endless ways to effectively impact a change in the law. Start by getting involved and seeking which area feels like a best fit for you. You will find that we can accomplish more together than we ever could apart.

Stop the Money Flow

Our system has proven that it cannot carry out unbiased justice with money as the end of all the means. Crime should not be a big business industry that heartless billionaires and investors reap from; rather, it should be a correctional system that helps troubled individuals recognize their harm to society and reintegrate back into society as a citizen prepared to succeed. For decades, our nation has epically failed at the opportunity to assist individuals in what should be a time of transformation for the greater good of everyone, but it's time to stop that now.

The first step in eliminating the money flow is to close down prison profiteering. The privatization of prisons only created the need for more prisons and more unregulated nonaccountable power systems that replicate inhumane and harsh treatments. Being understaffed and overcrowded to keep costs low and profits large has only escalated the current problem. The federal and state government needs to retain control of these facilities to phase out their use. Why am I telling you? Because you can play a part on any spectrum to help facilitate this change. Whether you sign a petition, lobby/protest your congressman/senators, or vote according to the parties that are in support of these endeavors, there is something you can do to cause change at all levels. Again, I'm leaving the responsibility to you to get involved in whatever way that works for you. If the dollars persist, so will the issue of mass incarceration. As stated earlier, money is the fuel that powers this engine to keep going. If the dollars dry up, so will the greedy characters that have turned incarceration into an industry.

Resource Allocation

Mass incarceration is a billion-dollar industry. Yet, inner city kids are hungry with no support outside of the school's free resources. Children that are too old for adoption agencies are left with no employment and nowhere to go, while our ineffective criminal justice system is one of the largest parts of our federal budget. There are no parks, recreation centers, kids' camps, or community resources, but prison systems are so well funded they have surplus for profit. As a nation, our priorities are out of order. We can positively and proactively change the current state of mass incarceration simply by resourcing funding allocation to build better and stronger communities.

The billions of dollars that are spent on ineffective prison systems could be reallocated to creating safe communities and healthy environments for children to receive the resources, attention, and education they need for survival. Many turn to crime as a means of survival, belonging, and identity. Some of these erroneous life choices can be mitigated with positive interventions. I can only wonder what the trajectory of my life would have been if I had a person that took intentional interest in my development through youth programs, mentorship, or providing a safe place for me to get free food and access to educational resources.

The federal funds that are being used to pay for prison systems can and should be reallocated to greater proactivity. Sure, many American citizens don't have a say in how federal funds are allocated, but many can and should exercise their power on local and state levels on how those funds are used. As a people, we must slowdown from the busyness of life and realize that we have more power than we think. Additionally, resource allocation doesn't only point to federal resources. If you have time, connections, education, finances, influence, affluence, or even a hobby that would edify impoverished people and communities, you share in the moral obligation to use it. There will always be needs and problems, and your contribution, in any form, can assist in providing solutions and advancement. Be one of the good characters in this narrative and find ways you can ignite change from where you are.

Change the Characters

There have been many characters who have played a role in advancing the systems that create mass incarceration. They have been exposed and their truest integrity revealed but, in most cases, never actually removed from their position of power. It's time to change characters.

The number one way to change characters through our system as it is requires voting. Some don't believe voting is effective, but it's a powerful act of unity and solidarity for or against one candidate, and their belief systems, or another. Besides, due to the present state of conditions, we have an emergency with nothing to lose. Voting requires more than participation at the ballot, but it requires attention to the people that are running for seats of office. There needs to be more vetting of their integrity, belief systems, and the behaviors that were taken from their previous position of power.

The other way to change characters is to *become* the character. Our nation is short of qualified, integral leaders that selflessly serve others. True leaders can lead from any place or position, as the criminal justice system is filled with the need for quality people that will uphold the standard of integrity with and without accountability. Our capitalist nature makes us think that we have to achieve the highest, most prestigious position in order to make an impact, but that is simply not true. Recall that I mentioned Dr. Benson? He was a life-changing, impactful leader that has continued to leave an impression on me. There are people in this world that will never know his name, but they will witness the fruit of his seed because they are growing and producing in me. And simply put, that could be you. You could become a character, at any role, on any level, and make life-changing generational shifts, whether the world knows your name or not. Maybe your call is to help change the character by becoming one, or at least, preparing to fill the seat when they are open.

Do Your Part

The sentencing project provides a list of specific starting points that are great to move the conversation from theory to action. You might be on the side of the spectrum that raises awareness, or you might be on the power side to enact direct change. No matter where you find yourself, think through these ideas as you go about doing your part:

- Eliminating mandatory minimum sentences and cutting back on excessively lengthy sentences; for example, by imposing a 20-year maximum on prison terms.
- Shifting resources to community-based prevention and treatment for substance abuse.
- Investing in interventions that promote strong youth development and respond to delinquency in age-appropriate and evidence-based ways.
- Examining and addressing the policies and practices, conscious or not, that contribute to racial inequity at every stage of the justice system.
- Removing barriers that make it harder for individuals with criminal records to turn their lives around.

I've given five major areas of change, but I don't want you to feel like these are the only areas. Think long and creatively so that you are a part of the solution that our world needs to see. There is so much room for growth and development for criminal justice that no effort of yours will be wasted.

It is my hope that this work has left you informed and charged to change. Our system is in a dire crisis state, and millions of people are impacted by it daily. I am one of the masses who lives to tell the story, and I will not stop my pursuit now that I've found my voice. It is no secret that corrections ain't correctin', that equity is being substituted for partial equality, at best, and the 13th amendment is responsible for the scheme that is being revealed generation by generation. It is my desire that you join me in every effort to see to it that young, black boys aren't lost to a system and to generations because of the ugly facade of prison as we know it. As I continue to fight for a fair trial and freedom, join me by doing your part to provide true justice for all.

CHAPTER 9:
FROM A BROTHA TO ANOTHER

"The opposite of poverty isn't wealth but instead is justice."
- Bryan Stevenson

There are times in life where we need people to tell us the raw, unadulterated, unfabricated truth. It's ugly and it doesn't feel good, but it's exactly what's needed. Think about this free game I'm about to give as that medicine you hate to taste so much but it's going to make everything feel better if you take it.

I know you've heard of keeping it real, and that's exactly what I aim to do here. The previous chapter's call to action applies to all of us. We all have a part to play in transforming this system. However, this section is specifically for those who identify as a black American. Our families, communities, economic impact, and generational wealth and existence are at stake here. We need to be on the forefront of leading this change so that one in every three black boys don't have to face prison in their lifetime, and simultaneously attack the rising number of black women that are entering prison with longer stays. We can play a major part in our freedom, so hear my heart and my direction as I see this as the best and most effective measure we have to drive change for the future of power.

POWER VS. POVERTY

Because we are the future of power, we must focus on what we can control. We have an obligation to care for and be intentional about the next generation. The fastest and most effective way to cease populating prisons with young black men and women is to intervene before negative influences lead them down paths that could get them caught in bad jams. I say *jams* literally and figuratively, because our music and pop culture has an extremely negative affect on our young people's perception of reality. The use and dealing of drugs coupled with objectifying and oversexualizing women's bodies glorifies the toxic culture and lifestyle choices that could easily get a young person entangled in the criminal justice system. We must take ownership and pride in loving our children to life and guiding them towards paths of success and progression. We cannot allow phones, Tik Tok, social media, and their electronic devices to hold the final say in where their destiny is and where it's going. We must do our parts in exposing our children to the vast largeness and beauty that our world beholds. If mass incarceration rates continue at their current rate, there will be a significant decrease in the existence of black and brown people. Mass incarceration can easily become mass genocide if we don't directly intervene and stop feeding the beast.

The Black Representative

I really respect the right to vote, and I understand why it's so important we push to go vote. It's both valuable and necessary, but it is no longer enough. I want the current and future generations to hear this loud and clear:

DON'T JUST VOTE BUT EDUCATE YOURSELF ON THE ISSUES AND RUN FOR OFFICE.

The only way we can truly change these oppressive laws is by changing our lawmakers. Voting is no longer enough by itself. To properly represent our hardships and deferred circumstances, we need someone in those seats of power that can speak up in a room full of peers on behalf of the struggles that the invisible system deals us daily. It's extremely difficult to represent the minority and disadvantaged communities when you've never been a part of those communities in any capacity. It's insane that there are people making financial and planning decisions for communities and people they have no relation to whatsoever. We cannot afford for lawmakers to continue selling the American dream while making prison the American reality of black people. Change from this narrative will ultimately happen when we change the lawmakers. You can be the voice of relation and power to bring the fullness of advocacy and equity to those areas.

Voting is your individual right, but a political seat gives you much more power than your singular vote. We deserve to have proper representation at all levels of law, and that representation could be you. It's high time we move from the ballot *only* to taking a seat at the conversation and decision-making table. This is a surefire way for the next generation to become the change we all wish to see. No one is saying that the road to political placement will be easy. I can't name one person in the world that would willingly give up their power. American history is inundated with racial and political ties, but it's nothing that can't be overcome. It will take grit, determination, and a passion like no other, but it is possible. We can move from teaching our children to "vote for the lesser of the evil," and become the good that our criminal justice system needs. More importantly, our young black men and women need us to be change-agents, interventionists, and revolutionaries at all levels of society. The law is a critical starting point. The law and those in the land are waiting for their law-changers. If we change the lawmakers, we change the laws.

RIVERA L. PEOPLES

I'm Still Not Free

Utmost respect for who I see,
The Man in the mirror looking back at me
but I'm still not free.
Born into poverty
In Nashville Tennessee, it was the early 90's when I use to
wonder if anybody really cared about me.
13 years..
162 months..
707 weeks..
4,953 days..
118,972 hours..
26 minutes.. I have been waiting for relief,
Done wrong in the name of Justice and I'm still not
free.
Arrested when I was 18 years young
Sentenced to Life plus 100 years
I can't say I was shocked cause it never seemed real.
Had all my constitutional rights violated just to convict me of
every charge that could've been thrown at me.
No, Not being a killer or even a criminal but criminal
responsibility
Could you handle the truth it's
closely told through the proof?
Justice for all unless they look like me and you
Through it all, my flaws and all
I overcame my charge and made my mom proud of me
Yet, I'm still not free.
In fact, she told me I'm everything she wished I'd be
A great father, paralegal, and an author
But I'm still not free.

When I checked my history books, I was not shocked to see my father, nor his forefathers were free.

Way before the 90's, my quest to be free would be met by Governor Lamar Alexander and his private interest in a check.

While under Lamar Alexander's control of the Tennessee Governor's mansion and the legislative branch, in 1983.

Corporate Corrections of America was also born in Nashville, Tennessee.

Private prison for profit was the beginning of why a lot of people who look like me would never be free.

Instead of using the state budget to invest in poverty, education, and those who look like me, Lamar and his political friends invested in prisons, lock 'em up and throw away the key. Creating a pipeline to prison and no we are still not free.

I now understand Frederick Douglas's speech titled, "What does the fourth of July mean to the slave?".

My father's fathers were in chains, plantations or prisons slavery by another name.

I'm still not free.

Injustice on every corner

Propaganda on every news channel

And it's not just me but, actually 1 in every 3 that's still not free.

This system has been broken from the very beginning and we all know it but why does it feel fixed?

Wait, I'll give you a hint.

Those in power have made a lot of generational wealth off it.
And no, I'm still not free.
I've followed the money,
Gotten to the scheme just to find out mass incarceration is
truly just Power vs. Poverty.
#Free my body
#Free R. [our] Peoples
#Free our culture

Life After Mass Incarceration Preview

Life After Mass Incarceration is a projected sequel to *Power vs. Poverty.* I am more than elated to release my post incarceration experiences to you in *Life After Mass Incarceration. Power vs. Poverty* centers on my lived experiences as incarcerated in some of the state of Tennessee's worst prisons. I share some of the best realizations and worst moments of my life while providing data that unveils the system of mass incarceration.

Now, can you imagine the first welcome home after these experiences? Or that warm embrace I get to give my children? Taking them to school and being a part of their extracurricular events? *Life After Mass Incarceration* will discuss my personal victories and challenges and the work my I have committed my life to.

I would be remiss to allow the triumph of injustice to stop with me. The vision I have for my freedom goes so much deeper, farther, and wider than circumstances. I will not wait until I am on the other side of these bars to begin transforming lives and impacting others. *Power vs. Poverty* is the beginning of a lifelong journey of selflessness, correcting misinformation, redirection through education, and generational impact. I aspire so much for my community, marginalized communities, and generations to come.

What you can expect
Faith and Family

Life After Mass Incarceration will journey through my experiences readjusting to societal norms and ways of living. I'll discuss the joys and sorrows of reacclimating myself as father, brother, friend, and citizen. Currently, there is no rehabilitation for these measures, but my family serves as an instrumental resource to keep me abreast of world changes.

Nonprofit

My life after mass incarceration will consist of working for the Non-Profit that I have started (at the time of this publication). My nonprofit was formed for the purpose of positively impacting at-risk youth by providing them a sturdy foundation. I was not given the tools, resources, information, and mentorship support that I needed, and I want to be able to provide that for others. Education is the basis of the programs that have been designed to provide hope and redirection to the inner-city youth we are seeking to target. I look forward to being actively involved in the lives of each and every youth we are blessed to serve.

Freeing R. [our] Peoples

The State of Tennessee has witnessed changes to the law that make it *slightly* harder to mass incarcerate. However, there is so much more work to be done. I desire that young people don't get entangled in any part, to any measure, with this system of oppression. I know that educational reform is the freedom our people need.

My life after mass incarceration will consist of fighting to transform educational laws and policies that permeate the school-to-prison pipeline while also fostering community awareness of such systems. Ignorance, coupled with the oppressive struggles of poverty, are killing generations of people. They are blind to the systematic traps that deepen their oppression, but they are also blind to the power that having knowledge can provide. I desire to change this. My ultimate goal is to defeat mass incarceration with mass education.

This book will be an autobiography of my successes and struggles to fulfill my life's mission. Journey with me through the coming pages as my path to freedom becomes the gateway to set others free.

REFERENCES

Due to the nature of website links to expiring, it is best to follow the citation for reference checks. At the time of publication, all links are valid and accessible.

Evan Knox Foreword 1 References

1.Foreword, by Cornell West p. xlvii The New Jim Crow by Michelle Alexander 10th anniversary edition

2. Powernomics: The national plan to empower black America by Chad Anderson chapter 1: racism, monopolies, and inappropriate behavior p.3

3. "IBID" p.5

4. https://www.prisonlegalnews.org/news/2022/mar/1/jpay-founder-ryan-shapiro-indicted-securities-fraud/

Chapter 1: What Is It?

1. World Prison Brief, Highest to Lowest Prison Population Rates
https://www.prisonstudies.org/highest-to-lowest/prison_population_rate?field_region_taxonomy_tid=All

2. Austin, J.; Coventry, G. (2001, February) Emerging Issues On Privatized Prisons
https://www.ojp.gov/pdffiles1/bja/181249.pdf

3.   American Civil Liberties Union. Mass Incarceration
https://www.aclu.org/issues/smart-justice/mass-
incarceration

4.   American Civil Liberties Union. Mass Incarceration
https://www.aclu.org/issues/smart-justice/mass-
incarceration

5.   Slavery By Another Name. Convict Leasing
https://www.pbs.org/tpt/slavery-by-another-
name/themes/convict-leasing/

6.   Slavery By Another Name. Convict Leasing
https://www.pbs.org/tpt/slavery-by-another-
name/themes/convict-leasing/

7.   Fair Fight Initiative. The History, Causes, and Facts
on Mass Incarceration
https://www.fairfightinitiative.org/the-history-causes-
and-facts-on-mass-incarceration/

8.   Fair Fight Initiative. The History, Causes, and Facts
on Mass Incarceration
https://www.fairfightinitiative.org/the-history-causes-
and-facts-on-mass-incarceration/

9.   Fair Fight Initiative. The History, Causes, and Facts
on Mass Incarceration
https://www.fairfightinitiative.org/the-history-causes-
and-facts-on-mass-incarceration/

10.   Durose, Matthew R., and Antenangeli, Leonardo

(2021,July). Recidivism of Prisoners Released in 34 States in 2012: A 5-Year Follow-Up Period (2012–2017).
https://bjs.ojp.gov/library/publications/recidivism-prisoners-released-34-states-2012-5-year-follow-period-2012-2017

11.   Benecchi, L. (2021, August) Recidivism Imprisons American Progress
https://harvardpolitics.com/recidivism-american-progress/

12.   Fair Fight Initiative. The History, Causes, and Facts on Mass Incarceration
https://www.fairfightinitiative.org/the-history-causes-and-facts-on-mass-incarceration/

13.   Corrections Corporation of America. (2022)
https://www.referenceforbusiness.com/history2/76/Corrections-Corporation-of-America.html

14.   Beasley, T. A New Industry Emerges To Meet A Very Real Need
https://www.corecivic.com/about/history

15.   Beasley, T. A New Industry Emerges To Meet A Very Real Need
https://www.corecivic.com/about/history

16.   Corrections Corporation of America. (2022)
https://www.referenceforbusiness.com/history2/76/Corrections-Corporation-of-America.html

17. Austin, J.; Coventry, G. (2001, February) Emerging Issues On Privatized Prisons

https://www.ojp.gov/pdffiles1/bja/181249.pdf

18. Galinato, Gregmar (2020, September) Privatized prisons lead to more inmates, longer sentences, study finds
https://news.wsu.edu/press-release/2020/09/15/privatized-prisons-lead-inmates-longer-sentences-study-finds/#:~:text=Privatized%20prisons%20lead%20to%20more%20%20inmates%2C%20longer%20sentences%2C%20study%20finds,-September%20%2015%2C%202020&text=When%20states%20turn%20to%20private,the%20length%20%20%20of%20sentences%20increases.&text=The%20study%20found%20that%20private,p%20er%20million%20population%20per%20year

19. Galinato, G.; Ryne, R. (2020, December) Do privately owned prisons increase incarceration rates?

https://doi.org/10.1016/j.labeco.2020.101908

20. Austin, J.; Coventry, G. (2001, February) Emerging Issues On Privatized Prisons

https://www.ojp.gov/pdffiles1/bja/181249.pdf

21. The White House. Executive Order on Reforming Our Incarceration System to Eliminate the Use of Privately Operated Criminal Detention Facilities

https://www.whitehouse.gov/briefingroom/presiden-
al-actions/2021/01/26/executive-order-reforming-
our-incarceration-system-to-eliminate-the-use-of-
privately-operated-criminal-detention-facilities/

22. Bureau of Justice Statistics. Recidivism and
Reentry

https://bjs.ojp.gov/topics/recidivism-and-reentry

Chapter 3: The Scheme Revealed

1. Corrections Corporation of America. (2022)
https://www.referenceforbusiness.com/history2/76/
Corrections-Corporation-of-America.html

2. States of Incarceration
https://statesofincarceration.org/story/cca-co-
founder-tom-beasley-nearby-smith-county

3. National Governors Association
https://www.nga.org/governor/lamar-alexander/

4. National Governors Association
https://www.nga.org/governor/lamar-alexander/

5. States of Incarceration
https://statesofincarceration.org/story/cca-
cofounder-tom-beasley-nearby-smith-county

6. States of Incarceration

https://statesofincarceration.org/story/cca-co-founder-tom-beasley-nearby-smith-county

7. Freeman, A. (1998, September) Tennessee Prison Privatization Bill Fails to Pass
    https://www.prisonlegalnews.org/news/1998/sep/15/tennessee-prison-privatization-bill-fails-to-pass/

8. Freeman, A. (1998, September) Tennessee Prison Privatization Bill Fails to Pass
    https://www.prisonlegalnews.org/news/1998/sep/15/tennessee-prison-privatization-bill-fails-to-pass/

9. Encyclopedia of Arkansas
    https://encyclopediaofarkansas.net/entries/terrell-don-hutto-12346/

10. Bauer, S. (2018, September) The True History of America's Private Prison Industry
    https://time.com/5405158/the-true-history-of-americas-private-prison-industry/

Chapter 4: Why does this matter?

1. Jubitana, C. (2019, May) Broken Hearts and Broken Homes: How Mass Incarceration Impacts Children and Families
    https://kenan.ethics.duke.edu/broken-hearts-and-broken-homes-how-mass-incarceration-impacts-children-and-families-may/

2.   Jane Addams College of Social Work. Mass Incarceration: Punishing the Families https://socialwork.uic.edu/news-stories/mass-incarceration-punishing-the-families/

3.   Scommegna, P. (2017, March) Studies Document Mass Incarceration's Toll On Families https://www.prb.org/resources/mass-incarcerations-toll-on-families/

4.   Jubitana, C. (2019, May) Broken Hearts and Broken Homes: How Mass Incarceration Impacts Children and Families https://kenan.ethics.duke.edu/broken-hearts-and-broken-homes-how-mass-incarceration-impacts-children-and-families-may/

Chapter 5: Equity

1.   Matt. 26:11

2.   https://www.merriamwebster.com/dictionary/poverty

3.   Consumer Financial Protection Bureau. Justice-Involved Individuals and the Consumer Financial Marketplace (2021, January) https://files.consumerfinance.gov/f/documents/cfpb_jic_report_2022-01.pdf

4.   Rabuy, B., Kopf, D. (2015, July) Prisons of Poverty: Uncovering the pre-incarceration incomes of the imprisoned

https://www.prisonpolicy.org/reports/income.html

5.   Nellis, Ashley, Ph.D. (2021) The Color of Justice: Racial and Ethnic Disparity in State Prisons https://www.sentencingproject.org/publications/color-of-justice-racial-and-ethnic-disparity-in-state-prisons/

6.   Rabuy, B., Kopf, D. (2015, July) Prisons of Poverty: Uncovering the pre-incarceration incomes of the imprisoned

https://www.prisonpolicy.org/reports/income.html

7.   NAACP. Criminal Justice Fact Sheet

https://naacp.org/resources/criminal-justice-fact-sheet

8.   Sawyer, W. (2020, July) Visualizing the racial disparities in mass incarceration

https://www.prisonpolicy.org/blog/2020/07/27/disparities/

9.   Bruce Western, Punishment and Inequality in America (New York: Russell Sage Foundation, 2006); Caroline Wolf Harlow, Education and Correctional Populations (Washington, D.C.: Bureau of Justice Statistics, 2003).

10.   Becky Pettit, Bryan Sykes, and Bruce Western, "Technical Report on Revised Population Estimates

and NLSY79 Analysis Tables for the Pew Public Safety and Mobility Project" (Harvard University, 2009).

Chapter 6: The 14 Amend(ed)

1. Federal Register. Annual Determination of Average Cost of Incarceration Fee (2021, September) https://www.federalregister.gov/documents/2021/09/01/2021-18800/annual-determination-of-average-cost-of-incarceration-fee-coif

2. Wendy, S. (2019, October) How race impacts who is detained pretrial https://www.prisonpolicy.org/blog/2019/10/09/pretrial_race/

3. Pretrial Detention: Harmful and Ineffective (2019, May) https://givingcompass.org/article/pretrialdetention-harmful-and-ineffective?landingPage=%2Ftopics%2Fcriminal-justice

4. Sawyer, Wendy and Wagner, Peter (2022, March) Mass Incarceration: The Whole Pie https://www.prisonpolicy.org/reports/pie2022.html

5. Cornell Law School. Legal Information Institute https://www.law.cornell.edu/wex/criminal_justice

6. University of Massachusetts Global. What is criminal justice? Investigating its purpose and professions

    https://www.umassglobal.edu/news-and-events/blog/what-is-criminal-justice

7. NAACP. Criminal Justice Fact Sheet

    https://naacp.org/resources/criminal-justice-fact-sheet

Chapter 7: Recidivism Rates

1. National Institute of Justice. Recidivism

    https://nij.ojp.gov/topics/corrections/recidivism#:~:text=Recidivism%20is%20one%20of%20the,intervention%20for%20a%20previous%20crime.

2. Chang, Dae (1977) FUNCTIONS OF CRIMINAL JUSTICE - PROCEDURES, TASKS AND PERSONNEL (FROM FUNDAMENTALS OF CRIMINAL JUSTICE - A SYLLABUS AND WORKBOOK, 1977, 2D ED.

    https://www.ojp.gov/ncjrs/virtual-library/abstracts/functions-criminal-justice-procedures-tasks-and-personnel

3. Benecchi, L. (2021, August) Recidivism Imprisons American Progress

https://harvardpolitics.com/recidivism-american-progress/

4. Benecchi, L. (2021, August) Recidivism Imprisons American Progress https://harvardpolitics.com/recidivism-american-progress/

5. Number of committed crimes in the United States in 2020, by type of crime https://www.statista.com/statistics/202714/number-of-committed-crimes-in-the-us- by-type-of-crime/#professional

6. Antenangeli, Leonardo, and Durose, Matthew R. (2021, September). Recidivism of Prisoners Released in 24 States in 2008: A 10-Year Follow-Up Period (2008–2018). https://bjs.ojp.gov/library/publications/recidivism-prisoners-released-24-states-2008-10-year-follow-period-2008-2018

7. Coulute, Lucius and Kopf, Daniel (2018, July) Out of Prison & Out of Work: Unemployment among formerly incarcerated people https://www.prisonpolicy.org/reports/outofwork.html

8. Labor force statistics from the current population survey. (2022). https://www.bls.gov/cps/

9. American Civil Liberties Union. (2022). https://www.aclu.org/issues/smart-justice/re-entry

10.   The United States Department of Justice Archives. (2017). https://www.justice.gov/archives/prison-reform

Chapter 9: A Call to Action

1.   Schneider, Andrea Kupfer and Alkon, Cynthia (2020, January) Our Criminal Legal System: Plagued by Problems and Ripe for Reform https://www.americanbar.org/groups/dispute_resolution/publications/dispute_resolution_magazine/2020/dr-magazine-criminal-justice-reform/our-criminal-legal-system/

Image References

Picture 1.

https://www.tennessean.com/story/news/2021/04/20/corecivic-lawsuitprivate-prison-operator-settle-56-million/7302711002/

Picture 2.
https://www.mtsu.edu/first-amendment/post/3219/judgelimitslawyer-s-tweets-about-tenn-prison-firm-he-s-suing

Picture 3.
https://www.prisonpolicy.org/profiles/TN.html

Picture 4.

https://mobile.twitter.com/danielahorwitz

https://m.facebook.com/hartsville.tn.prison/

https://mobile.twitter.com/danielahorwitz

https://www.prisonlegalnews.org/news/2019/jul/16/corecivic-
prisonstennessee-have-twice-many-murders-four-times-
homiciderate-staterun-facilities/

Picture 5.
https://m.facebook.com/hartsville.tn.prison/

https://m.facebook.com/hartsville.tn.prison/

Picture 6.
https://www.nashvillescene.com/news/pithinthewind/2021-
in-
prisondeaths/article_a7d90aec-6a5c-11ec-
a8e8eb9f86672043.html

https://m.facebook.com/hartsville.tn.prison/

https://m.facebook.com/hartsville.tn.prison/
https://m.facebook.com/hartsville.tn.prison/

Picture 7.
https://www.tennessean.com/story/news/2018/08/06/nashv
illecorecivic-private-prisons-
headquartersentrancesblockedprotesters/912735002/

https://www.nashvillescene.com/news/pithinthewind/protes
ters-haveput-corecivics-headquarters-on-
lockdown/article_5fcb7f20066c-51d3ba35-
ed5aada3ec7f.html

Picture 8.
https://m.facebook.com/hartsville.tn.prison/

Picture 9.
https://m.facebook.com/hartsville.tn.prison/

Picture 10
https://dailymemphian.com/article/32029/tennessees-privateprison-operator-corecivic-ramps-up-campaign-spending-election

Picture 11 https://wpln.org/post/tennessee-lawmakers-pass-truth-insentencing-bill-following-months-of-heated-debate/

ACKNOWLEDGEMENTS

When I don't know where to begin, I always start with God. A long time ago, I promised God, not if, but when I make it out of this mess, I will do whatever it takes to keep someone else from coming into a system like this. I also promised I'll do whatever I can to help someone get out of a situation like mine. This book and my paralegal certificate allows me to keep my promise in advance. So for that, I thank and acknowledge God for never putting more on me than I could bear.

Curtis "Wall Street" Carroll,

Your story inspired me in ways I never knew I could be inspired (I certainly recommend looking him up).

William Green #470814,

My brother, I watched you write, publish, and put your all in a dope poem book titled, "Striving Struggle Of A Juvenile Growing Grown In A System." Thanks for leading the way and showing me this was possible and could be done. I love you. Like your mom always says, "SMILE!!"

My guy Big Fridge, sometimes known as Calvin Bryant #451242,

Calvin Bryant, my mentor Once known as inmate #451242 aka Big Fridge. I've seen you carry high school defenders on your back while scoring touchdowns for Hillsboro, I've seen you carry the entire sport of Nashville high school football into it's glory days on your back, I've seen you carry your families legacy on your back. I've seen you carry a unjust conviction and sentence on your back while walking the prison yard with me at Charles Bass Correctional Facility, and Northwest Correctional Facility with "TN Department of Corrections" written on your back literally. I've seen No Name attorneys turned into House Hold names off your back. I seen you fight tirelessly over a decade not just for your freedom, but EVERYONE negatively effected by Tennessee erroneous, unconstitutional, and discriminatory drug free school zone law and I seen you humbly walk out of prison not blaming anyone for the decade of injustice you experienced. I've seen you dedicate your life to a much bigger purpose. I seen you become the father you always said you'd be. I seen the positive impact you have had on inner city kids. I listened to your advice, I felt your encouraging words and because I did my life is on a much greater trajectory. Nashville is lucky to call you our own. Keep us on your back or we'll fall off bad like Nashville high school football did without you lol.. but in all seriousness God blessed your heart to bless others and you have not disappointed. Carry on Fridge.

Brandon "Amire" Adams,

I'm forever indebted. Rain, sleet, hail, or snow, I knew I could find you in the law library waiting on me.

Daniel Pettigrew AKA Spazz #562960,

I can honestly say this book would've never happened had we not talked as much as we did. Your love for books was the only tool I had at my disposal as I embarked on this journey. May your light continue to shine bright and keep kicking Parkinson's ass.

Ropa my G, Terrence Smith #299127

The guidance, and knowledge you shared with me from the very beginning is still a part of my growth today.

Chico da don aka Kevin Wilson #262828

You have always been as solid as a rock, and standing strongly upon everything you believe in; they should make an award for that.

P, Teddie, and Pretty Black

It'll take an entirely separate book to mention where we've been and where we're going.

Britt,

The world needs real friends like Britt Britt. From the cradle to the grave; Michael Phillips, we're locked in.
To my THEI family,
Supreme Gratitude to the entire THEI family. I am truly grateful for the life-changing educational experience. Thanks for the respect you give your student population.

To my niece Shatorria,

Your passion for art is something I always knew would take you far in this world. This cover illustration is something I'm so proud of because you were the first person to understand that I wanted people to judge my book by its cover. Thank you for being a part of my heart.

To my family,

Last, but certainly not least, you are my world. You all give me so much to stand up for, to fight for, to love, to miss, and to fight for some more. Without the love for my family, I would have never stayed strong.

Dear Pops,

I'm thankful for everything you do for me, my brother, & sister. Even without you being here you still make your presence felt in our lives every way you can. You always find a way to provide for us no matter what. Your someone we can talk to about anything. I can't wait for you to come home.

I love u, Kameron

Daddy, I love and miss you so much. I am so ready for you to come home. thank you for always being there for me whenever I need you.

<3 Skylar

You're the best dad anyone could ask for. Your always there when we need you. You make sure we get what we need, and you always find a way to reward us for our good grades. I can't wait for you to come home with us.

Love, Zay

FREE OUR PEOPLES
FOR ALL THOSE WHO HAVE BEEN CONVICTED
BY OUR PEOPLES SO...